A Family Money-

Divorce and Separation

A Family Money-Go-Round
Special

Divorce and Separation

Felicity White

Series editor
Richard Northedge

Telegraph Publications

Published by Telegraph Publications
135 Fleet Street, London EC4P 4BL

First published in 1987

© Daily Telegraph 1987

This book is sold subject to the condition that it shall not, by way of trade or otherwise, be lent, re-sold, hired out or otherwise circulated without the publisher's prior consent in any form of binding or cover other than that in which it is published.

All rights reserved. No part of this work may be reproduced or transmitted by any means without permission.

Photoset by Rowland Phototypesetting Ltd, Bury St Edmunds, Suffolk
Printed and bound in Great Britain by Biddles Ltd, Guildford and King's Lynn

British Library Cataloguing in Publication Data
White, Felicity
Divorce and Separation – (A Family Money-Go-Round Special)
1. Divorce – England
I. Title   II. Series
306.8'9'0942   HQ876

ISBN 086367 097 0

For
AARB

Acknowledgements

I would like to thank Anna Mumford for her patience in editing this book and Timothy Scott, family law barrister, for his invaluable advice and support. I acknowledge that any errors and omissions are entirely my own responsibility.

Felicity J. White

Felicity White

Contents

Introduction 11

Chapter 1. Reconciliation or divorce? 13
Reconciliation – how to find help 13
Do you need a solicitor? 15
How to find a suitable solicitor 16
What to expect from a solicitor 17
The first interview 17

Chapter 2. Separation and divorce proceedings – the grounds and the courts 21
The six-month reconciliation period 23
Undefended divorce 24
The financial application in the petition 28
The claim for custody in the petition 30
Defended divorce 31
Hitches and hurdles 32
Judicial separation 33
Deed of separation 33

Chapter 3. How to handle your own divorce proceedings 35
The procedure 35
Children 37
Finance 37

Chapter 4. Looking after the children 39
Conciliation 39
Joint custody 40
Sole custody 40

Care and control 41
Access 42
Travelling abroad with the children 43
Change of name 44
Disputes over custody, care and control, and access 44
Child abduction 47

Chapter 5. Violence – protection for the family 53
Taking action against violence 53
Contact a solicitor as soon as you can 54
Obtaining an injunction 54

Chapter 6. The financial arrangements 57
The financial application 57
Consent orders 61
Family Law Bar Association (FLBA) Conciliation Board 61
Maintenance 62
Tax implications of maintenance orders 65
Fixing a sum for maintenance 68
Financial provision in the magistrates court 72
Debts and liabilities 73
The alimony drone – myth or reality? 75
The matrimonial home 78
Household contents 83
Other capital assets 84
Capital gains tax 85
Capital transfer tax/inheritance tax 86
Financial relief – the foreign element 87

Chapter 7. Other financial provisions 89
Loss of pension rights on divorce 89
Death-in-service benefit 90
Insurance policies 90
Education 91
Wills 92

Chapter 8. The unmarried couple 93
Ownership of property 93
Supplementary benefit 95
Maintenance 95
The Inheritance (Provision for Family and Dependants) Act 96

Chapter 9. Coping with legal costs 97
Taxation of a bill 98

Legal aid 99
Orders for costs in court proceedings 105
Are you entitled to state benefits? 106
Supplementary benefit 106
Family income supplement 107

Chapter 10. Scotland and Ireland 109
Divorce proceedings in Scotland and Northern Ireland 109
Scotland 109
The position in Northern Ireland 111

Appendices 113
A List of useful addresses 113
B Solicitors' Family Law Association Code of Practice 117
C Sample forms 121
D Deed of Separation 127
E List of conciliation services 129
F Legal Aid information 136
G Checklist for income 138

Index 141

Introduction

All the books in this series concern money. Not all the books concern joyous occasions however. This one is about divorce and separation, and however amicable the parting, it is an admission that plans entered into with hope have failed to be fulfilled. It is hardly surprising if there is bitterness on one side of the relationship at least, and possibly blame for one partner. Even discussing divorce rationally may be difficult.

Divorce is probably a harder process than marriage. Most people have few assets to pool when they wed, and they are not concerned with the equality of their contribution to the marital finances. By the time they think of separation there is likely to be a home of considerable value to which they can both lay claim, possibly some joint savings, one-thousand-and-one artifacts that may have been bought together and which only one can take – and children. One partner may have forfeited income to establish the relationship too.

If two people really can live for the cost of one, then it follows that separation raises their expenditure again.

And separation or divorce means sorting out pension rights, agreeing maintenance and adjusting the partners' tax positions. It is a daunting task at an inevitably difficult and emotional time, but it is one which has to be arranged carefully. For many people, being divorced lasts longer than their marriage.

Because of the importance of a divorce or separation and because of the permanence, the partners must be advised properly. As with buying a house, that almost inevitably means using a solicitor, which is partly why a member of the legal profession has been chosen for writing this book – but as with house buying, it is possible to avoid using a solicitor, and this book also explains the procedures involved in doing-it-yourself.

As with all the books in this series, the aim is not to make readers into experts themselves – particularly for an event which it must be hoped happens only once in a lifetime if it is to happen at all. The aim is to give the advice of experts. Some people may read the book from cover to cover; others only look at specific chapters which affect them, as they are affected. The book permits that and allows the reader to select those parts which deal with his or her problem. Many people will use the book as a back-up to the advice which they are paying their own solicitor to provide – and some will find it useful reading to understand better and offer solutions to friends with problems.

The Money-go-Round sections of the Daily Telegraph – which appear on Wednesdays as well as Saturdays – look regularly at the problems associated with divorce and separation. These constitute the broadest and most comprehensive personal finance sections to be found in any daily newspaper, but while such articles can look at the changes in the legal and taxation systems affecting partners who split up, and although they can discuss specific problems facing partners, it requires books such as these to collate the information and to explain it in greater detail in a permanent form.

The addition of a book on divorce and separation is a valuable extension to this series.

Richard Northedge
Deputy City Editor
Daily Telegraph

Chapter 1

Reconciliation or divorce?

At some time during their marriage many people will reach a point at which the possibility of separation and divorce enters their minds. For many people, this possibility will become a reality. These days there is a great deal of coverage about divorce in newspapers and on radio and television programmes. Marriage breakdown is no longer a taboo subject, nor a social stigma, and it has obtained a high profile in our society. Perhaps this is one of the reasons why, when something does go wrong in a marriage, the couple assume that separation and divorce is the only solution. This may very well be totally incorrect. There may be any number of reasons why you consider your marriage is breaking down. Perhaps a gulf in communication has developed between you and your partner; or there may be financial problems which are producing strains and tensions upon the relationship. Young children can be exhausting and time-consuming and this may also have taken its toll.

Reconciliation – how to find help

There is a great deal of help available to couples who are trying to sort out the problems in their marriage. If the decision at the end of the day is to go ahead with divorce proceedings, there are people available to help make your passage through those proceedings as easy as possible. The addresses and telephone numbers in Appendix A will give you a reference point from which to begin.

Marriage Guidance Council

Before you decide to take the first step towards consulting a solicitor to file divorce proceedings, consider and try to resolve the problems which have arisen between you and your spouse. Many couples arrange to consult a Marriage Guidance counsellor. The National Marriage Guidance Council was set up in 1937. In the early days, it used volunteers, many of whom were not specifically trained in the very delicate and important skill of counselling. However, it has moved quickly with the times and the training, which every counsellor is required to undertake, produces compassionate and highly-skilled personnel. You may have to wait a few weeks for an appointment, and you will be asked to make a modest contribution – though this is generally waived if you are in financial difficulty. The Marriage Guidance Council has branches throughout the country and your local Citizen's Advice Bureau will be able to give you the address and telephone number of your nearest one. Alternatively, the telephone directory will provide the information you require.

Most couples find it helpful to discuss the problems which have arisen during their marriage with the help of a third party who is a skilled counsellor. Even if the couple decide that the best course of action is to part, the discussions often enable the parting to be on a more amicable basis than it would have been had they not had the chance to air their feelings. An amicable separation is obviously preferable whatever the circumstances and especially where children are involved. It is not their fault that their parents are unable to live together as husband and wife; nor does separation or divorce mean that the couple cannot continue to be good parents.

Emotional trauma, to a greater or lesser degree, is an inevitable part of the process of separation and divorce. It is perfectly natural, and will affect even the most friendly separation and divorce. Psychiatrists have likened divorce to bereavement in that it is necessary for there to be a mourning period for the death of the marriage. It is not abnormal to experience such feelings and it always helps to talk about them with a friend, relative or experienced counsellor. The Marriage Guidance Council does not limit its work to the attempt to reconcile a marriage; it will also provide continuing support throughout the period of separation, divorce and beyond if it is needed.

Other counselling organisations

The Marriage Guidance Council is not the only option open to you. There are a number of organisations in England and Wales which provide skilled counselling and work towards the reconciliation of problems in a marriage and a greater understanding between the couple.

Consult Appendix E for a list of conciliation services and the address of the Institute of Family Therapy. These services offer not only counselling for reconciliation of the marriage, but also advice which might enable you and your partner to come to terms with disputes and reach agreement on issues relating to the children or any other matters.

There is a tendency for people to look upon counsellors as busybodies who will be accusatorial and admonitory. In fact, they are highly skilled at their craft and if you have these fears you will be pleasantly surprised by the help that they can give you. It is wise to think seriously about obtaining help and advice from the conciliation services before leaping headlong into the legal procedures which lead to divorce.

Mediator lawyers

At the moment there is a strong trend in the US towards using mediator lawyers. These are lawyers who have trained as mediators and can advise their clients in their capacity as mediator, lawyer or both. The idea of the mediator lawyer is under discussion in this country but as yet its practical application is at the embryonic stage. However, there is a strong trend among family lawyers in England and Wales to work towards a conciliatory approach which encourages the parties to discuss between them the problems and the arrangements to be made on separation and divorce. This leads to a calmer and friendlier atmosphere between the parties and decreases the acrimony which has been the hallmark of so many broken marriages in the past.

Do you need a solicitor?

Divorce by the special procedure is straightforward and it is quite possible for you to deal with the process and obtain a decree of divorce yourself. All county courts with divorce jurisdiction will supply you with the appropriate forms and written explanation as to how to go about petitioning for a divorce and obtaining a final decree of divorce without consulting a solicitor (see Chapter 3).

However, first a word of warning: consider carefully the value of consulting a solicitor for basic advice as to your rights and duties on separation and divorce. Even if you are in full agreement with your spouse with regard to the divorce proceedings, the financial arrangements and the arrangements for the children, it would be wise for both of you to consult solicitors who will check the agreement that the two of you have reached and ensure that both of you are aware of any pitfalls or unforeseen possibilities.

Most importantly of all, the solicitors will check that the agreement has been reached between you with full knowledge of each other's financial position. If you intend the financial agreement reached between you and your spouse to be binding, it is vital that there has been a full disclosure on both sides as to your income and capital position. Without this, there is always the possibility that the agreement may be reopened by the court if a material fact which has not been disclosed subsequently comes to light. Your solicitor will advise you as to whether the financial agreement reached between you should be incorporated into a court order or into a deed of separation; and should also be able to advise you how to proceed.

One fact to bear in mind if you choose not to consult a solicitor is that if things go wrong at a later date, you may find yourselves with greater legal costs to bear than you would had you consulted a solicitor in the first place. An hour with a solicitor seeking advice over the arrangements reached between you and your spouse may save you much time, emotional energy and expense at a later date.

Many people fear that consulting a solicitor may disrupt the delicately balanced agreement which they have reached with their spouse. To ensure this does not happen it is important to choose a solicitor who is a regular practitioner in the field of family law. Most good solicitors will be happy to find that you have dealt with many of the matters between yourselves on a friendly basis and will not seek to disrupt the agreement which you have reached or to drive a wedge between you and your spouse. Your solicitor cannot force you to take his advice and if, after listening to your solicitor's advice, you wish to disregard it you may of course do so.

How to find a suitable solicitor

Approximately four years ago, a number of solicitors practising in family law set up an association called The Solicitors' Family Law Association, which now has membership throughout England and Wales. The main function of this organisation is to maintain a list of solicitors who adhere to the Association's code of practice (see Appendix B).

The founding solicitors of The Solicitors' Family Law Association were perturbed by the adversarial, and sometimes aggressive, approach of family solicitors and the association was formed with a view to advocating the conciliatory approach towards family law. Although there can never be any guarantees, if you choose a solicitor who adheres to the code of practice of The Solicitors' Family Law Association, you should find an experienced and sympathetic ear. In addition, you will find a solicitor who is happy to advise you and to help you reach agreement with your spouse on all matters. The period of separation and divorce is a stressful and emotional time and it is at a time like this that you need not only sound advice but also a sympathetic ear. The secretary of The Solicitors' Family Law Association (see Appendix A) will provide you with a list of solicitors in your area who are members of the association.

If there are no members in your area, contact the Citizen's Advice Bureau and ask for the name of a solicitor who specialises in family/

matrimonial work. It is important to find a solicitor whose practice is substantially family law, and you will find that more and more solicitors are specialising in particular branches of the law. If the Citizen's Advice Bureau is unable to provide this information then the secretary of your local branch of the Law Society will certainly be able to help you. Telephone the Law Society in Chancery Lane, London (see Appendix A) and ask for the name and telephone number of your local branch.

What to expect from a solicitor

If, after consulting an experienced Marriage Guidance counsellor, there is no possibility of reconciliation within your marriage, it is likely that the next step you take will be to make an appointment with a solicitor. Many people are fearful of this step, believing that, once they have consulted a solicitor, they have made a move towards divorce from which there is no return. This is untrue. It is important to remember that it is your life and it is your divorce. If you decide, at any point, that you do not want to file divorce proceedings, make this clear to your solicitor. On the other hand, solicitors are there to advise you; make sure that you fully understand the consequences of your decision and the alternatives on offer before you commit yourself to any positive action. Most solicitors these days, far from being aloof, are eager to help you. They realise, above all, that it is vital that you understand what is happening.

The first interview

At first, your solicitor may talk to you about the problems which have occurred, and ask you if there are any prospects of reconciliation. Some solicitors feel that it is not their responsibility to enter into detailed discussion on these subjects. They might even take the view that you have come to them for divorce, and that is exactly what you will get. But these days, family law solicitors are usually ready to discuss problems and possible solutions with you; they are also anxious not to push you into a decision which you are not ready to make. Solicitors are becoming more and more aware of the psychological effect of marital problems and divorce, and of the emotional trauma which you might well be experiencing.

It is always extremely difficult to talk to a complete stranger about the most intimate details concerning the problems in your marriage. Many solicitors, when you make the appointment with them, will ask you to write to them giving basic details – the date of the marriage, your age, number of children, financial details (such as the income of you and your spouse), value of your home, amount and nature of your savings and so on. Sometimes, you will be asked to jot down what you think has gone wrong in the marriage, and what has led you to consult a solicitor at this time. Some people are happy with this method, preferring to write volumes to the solicitor and feel reassured that the solicitor will know practically the whole story before he or she even starts the interview. Other people feel constrained and unable to put anything but the barest financial details on paper before the meeting. Do whatever comes most naturally to you.

Generally, your solicitor will be anxious to put you at ease and to ensure that you feel able to ask any questions which arise. Most family solicitors offer their client a cup of tea or coffee, then start the interview by taking down basic details which will help them gain a picture of the family and its financial structure. This will also help you, the client, settle down and form some view about the solicitor and his or her approach. The information you will be asked to supply will vary according to how much you supplied in advance. However, it will be along the following lines:

(a) Full names of yourself and your spouse;
(b) Address of yourself and your spouse;
(c) Date of marriage;
(d) Place of marriage;
(e) Occupation of your spouse;
(f) Your occupation;
(g) Dates of birth and full names of all children;
(h) Details of previous marriage(s) of you and your spouse;
(i) Details of children of previous marriage(s);
(j) Nationality;
(k) Details of your family;
(l) Details of your spouse's family.

Your solicitor will also ask you for as much information as you can supply about the family finances, for example:

(a) Your income;
(b) Any benefits in kind from employment;
(c) Your partner's income;
(d) Any benefits which you or your spouse derive from employment, such as bonus, free lunches, company car, expense account;
(e) Any private income to which you or your spouse are entitled;
(f) Any income from any other source, such as any other business, employment or investment;
(g) A list of your capital assets;
(h) A list of your spouse's capital assets, including savings account,

bank deposit accounts, stocks, shares, houses, boats, jewellery, premium bonds etc;
(i) A list of insurance policies, property overseas, any other assets realisable or not;
(j) A list of debts: joint debts and debts in your sole name or your spouse's sole name, for example bank overdraft, Barclaycard debt, Access or any other credit card, HP agreement, loan agreement – secured or unsecured – department store charge card, and so on.

As well as trying to build up a full picture of the family finances, your solicitor will also want to know what has made you decide to consult a solicitor and what has gone wrong with the relationship, so as to advise you whether you have a basis on which to obtain a decree of divorce.

At the end of the first interview your solicitor will advise you of your statutory rights and duties and will usually give you some idea of what might be a likely financial arrangement and how that can be reached. Your solicitor should discuss with you the manner in which your spouse or spouse's solicitor should be approached and may well suggest marriage guidance or some form of counselling if you have not already considered it.

The first interview is also the time to discuss legal costs and eligibility for legal aid (see Chapter 9). You should be aware, before consulting a solicitor of the fixed-fee interview scheme.

The fixed-fee interview

This is a scheme whereby a solicitor will give you an appointment – generally for 30 minutes – at a fixed fee of £5. This fee is irrespective of your own financial resources. If you wish to make use of this scheme, you should ensure at the time you make the appointment that the solicitor you approach will see you for a fixed-fee interview. Many solicitors do not offer the scheme, mainly because 30 minutes is not nearly long enough properly and carefully to advise a client unless the client requires advice on a small and specific point. Also, the green form scheme (see Chapter 9), will cover the solicitor's costs on initial advice for a longer period.

Changing to a new solicitor

It is perfectly acceptable to change your solicitor if you are unhappy with his or her work, but if you are in receipt of the legal aid certificate, the Law Society, which runs the Legal Aid Scheme, will want to have a very good reason for your doing so, especially if it occurs too frequently.

It is your right to choose the person who is to advise you and represent you. No solicitor can force you to continue to instruct him or her, and if you are unhappy about the way your solicitor is conducting your case or if there is a personality clash then you may change to another solicitor. The procedure is simple. You choose a new solicitor, establish that this solicitor is prepared to act for you, and write to your previous solicitor requesting that he or she transfer your papers to your new solicitor.

If you are in receipt of a legal aid certificate, your previous solicitor will undoubtedly want you to settle any outstanding costs before he or she transfers the papers to the new solicitor.

Chapter 2

Separation and divorce proceedings – the grounds and the courts

There is one ground for divorce in this country and that is the irretrievable breakdown of the marriage. The court will grant a divorce only if this ground has been proved by one of the five following facts:

(a) That one spouse has committed adultery;
(b) That one spouse has behaved unreasonably;
(c) That one spouse has deserted the other for a period of at least two years;
(d) That the husband and the wife have been separated for a period of at least two years and the other spouse consents to a decree of divorce;
(e) That the husband and the wife have been separated for a period of at least five years. In this case the other spouse's consent to the divorce is not necessary.

A petition for divorce (see Appendix C) can be presented to the court at any time after the expiry of one year of marriage. It is either presented in almost any county court, or if you live in central London, at the Divorce Registry which is situated at Somerset House on the Strand. The spouse who presents the petition is known as the petitioner, while the recipient of the petition is called the respondent. You must fulfil the following conditions if you are to petition for a decree of divorce in England and Wales:

(a) You must have been married for at least one year;
(b) You or your spouse must be domiciled (see below) in England and Wales; or
(c) You must have been ordinarily resident in England and Wales for

a period of one year immediately preceding the presentation to the court of your petition for divorce.

Domicile is a complicated legal concept. Everyone has a domicile of origin, ie the place where they were born and this remains their domicile unless, and until, it is specifically changed by that person to a domicile of choice. When a person chooses to take up permanent residence in another country and the person decides that the chosen country is, from then on, their permanent home, this country will be defined in legal terms as their domicile of choice.

The approach

It is useful if your solicitor, before presenting a petition to the court, can write to your spouse if your spouse has not yet instructed a solicitor. The letter will invite your partner to consult a solicitor so that as much agreement on all the issues can be reached before a petition is filed. If such a letter can be written, it is obviously preferable for the respondent to receive this preliminary indication of his/her spouse's intention rather than suddenly receiving a formal and threatening petition. Alternatively, if your spouse has already consulted a solicitor, it is useful for your respective solicitors to discuss matters in order to try and take the heat out of the situation and obtain agreement on as much as possible before a petition is presented to the court. Discuss with your solicitor the basis on which your divorce petition will be presented to the court.

Adultery

If you decide to make an adultery allegation, you must state in the petition that the respondent has committed adultery with another person, who is known as the co-respondent. You must name the co-respondent if you know the name and if you do not, write 'a co-respondent whose name and identity is unknown to the petitioner'. If the co-respondent is known to you by one name only, say, Janet, you should state 'a co-respondent whose name and identity is known only as Janet'. You should state the dates on which and places where the adultery took place if you know these details. You must also state that you find it intolerable to live with the respondent.

Unreasonable behaviour

There is no formal definition of unreasonable behaviour. Violence to the petitioner or to the children of the family is one example. Excessive drinking, excessive work commitments, constant nagging, financial irresponsibility (for example, the build up of debts to the detriment of the family), and refusal to have sexual intercourse are further examples which can be cited in a petition of unreasonable behaviour. You should discuss your spouse's behaviour with your solicitor who will advise you how this should be dealt with in the petition. It is usual to make one or two general statements about the respondent's behaviour and to give specific instances of the respondent's unreasonable behaviour, giving brief details, dates and places.

You must prove, to the satisfaction of the court, that the respondent has behaved in such a way that you, as the petitioner, cannot reasonably be expected to live with him or her. If you and your spouse are still living under the same roof it is important to cite the most recent instances of unreasonable behaviour, certainly within the last six months.

Desertion
Desertion is rarely used but refers to a period of separation between the husband and wife of at least two years, where separation occurs against the wishes of one party.

Two years' separation
You must state in the petition that you and the respondent have lived separate and apart for a period of at least two years giving the date of separation as accurately as possible. The respondent must consent to a decree of divorce obtained on this basis.

It is possible to remain living under the same roof during this period of two years' separation but you must live 'separate and apart' (the technical term for living apart). You must not care for each other domestically, ie you each do your own washing, cooking, cleaning, shopping etc and you must, of course, sleep in separate rooms.

Five years' separation
If the respondent does not consent to a decree of divorce being granted on the basis of two years' separation then you must wait until you have lived separate and apart for five years (unless you can use an alternative ground) when the respondent's consent is not required. Again you must give the date of separation as accurately as possible.

There is a provision within divorce proceedings, based on five years' separation, for the respondent to stop the final decree on the ground that a decree of divorce would produce grave financial or other hardship to the respondent. In such cases, the court will not allow a final decree of divorce until the respondent's financial position after the divorce has been determined.

The six-month reconciliation period
Adultery
If a period of six months or more has expired from the date on which the petitioner first knew of the adultery to the date on which the

petition is presented to the court, the decree cannot be pronounced. The court considers that a six-month period in which the couple have continued to live together indicates that the petitioner has condoned and accepted the adultery.

Unreasonable behaviour

Living together for a period of six months or more since the date of the last alleged act of unreasonable behaviour would not automatically prevent a decree of divorce being pronounced, but the court would be likely to request an explanation, and may well conclude that the respondent's behaviour is not so unreasonable that the petitioner cannot be expected to live with the respondent.

Separation for two years and five years

Any period or periods of living together which last six months or less, will not prevent the pronouncement of a decree of divorce. However, the period will not count as part of the two years' or five years' separation.

Undefended divorce

The vast majority of divorce petitions are now undefended, mainly because of the financial and emotional expense of a defended action. An undefended divorce is one in which the respondent does not resist the divorce taking place. If your petition is not defended by your spouse you could expect your divorce to be finalised within four to five months. This period varies according to the speed with which your local county court deals with the administration of the divorce petition. Every county court, including the Divorce Registry, will provide you with the appropriate forms and information if you wish to conduct the proceedings yourself (see Chapter 3).

The passage of an undefended petition up to *decree nisi*

1. The procedure begins when the petition for divorce is filed at the county court together with a statement concerning the arrangements for the children, if there are children of the family (see Appendix C).
2. A petition fee of £40 together with the original marriage certificate and a certificate of reconciliation signed by the petitioner's solicitor are also lodged with the petition and statement concerning the arrangements for the children.
3. The statement of arrangements for the children provides information to the court about the children, ie their home address, a description of the property in which they live, where they are educated, and any decisions which have been taken with regard to the provision for access and maintenance (see Chapter 4).

4 The certificate of reconciliation is a certificate signed by your solicitor informing the court whether or not he or she has discussed reconciliation with you, and whether or not your solicitor has recommended an organisation like the Marriage Guidance Council, which may be able to help with reconciliation.

5 A copy of the petition and statement of arrangements for the children together with a form of acknowledgement of service (see Appendix C) will then be sent to the respondent or to the respondent's solicitor.

6 The form of acknowledgement of service must be completed by the respondent or his or her solicitor and lodged at the county court.

7 The acknowledgement of service states that the respondent has received the petition and indicates whether or not he or she intends either to defend the petition, or to make an application for financial relief, or to apply for custody and/or access to the children of the family, and whether or not there is any objection to the petitioner's claim that the respondent pay the costs of the divorce proceedings.

8 If adultery is alleged and a co-respondent is named, a copy of the petition together with a form of acknowledgement of service is also sent to the co-respondent to be completed and returned to the court.

9 The acknowledgement of service must be completed and returned to the court within eight days.

10 If the petition is based on the respondent's adultery, then the respondent is required to sign the acknowledgement of service personally, which constitutes admission to the adultery, and return it to the court. (If the respondent does not intend to defend the petition.)

11 If the petition is based on two years' separation then the respondent is required to give assent to the question. 'Do you consent to a decree of divorce?' and to sign the acknowledgement of service personally.

12 In the case of an unreasonable behaviour petition, a desertion petition and a petition based on five years' separation it is quite correct for the respondent's solicitor to complete and sign the acknowledgement of service returning it to the court within the specified eight days.

13 The court will send a sealed photocopy of the acknowledgement of service to the petitioner or the petitioner's solicitor, thus indicating that the petitioner can proceed with the next step, an application for 'directions for trial'. The petitioner will complete a form described as a request for directions for trial (special procedure)

together with an affidavit in support of the request and a copy of the acknowledgement of service attached (or technically known as exhibited) to the affidavit. These documents are then lodged at the court, where they will go before a registrar who will check that everything is in order. If it is, the registrar will notify both the petitioner and the respondent of a date for the pronouncement of *decree nisi*, the first decree of divorce.

The affidavit in support of the petition

An affidavit is a document which is sworn in front of a commissioner for oaths, a solicitor, or an official at the court office. People with no religious belief can 'affirm' the affidavit. There is a statutory fee of £3 per affidavit and 75 pence per exhibit if the documents are sworn before a commissioner of oaths or a solicitor. There is no fee for swearing either document before an official of the court.

The affidavit in support of the petition is a simple document in question form (see Appendix C). There is a separate affidavit in support of each of the five facts upon which a petition can be presented.

Affidavit in support of an adultery petition

You must state, once again, the facts upon which you based your allegation of adultery, the date on which and the circumstances in which the adultery first became known to you. If the respondent has admitted the adultery you should exhibit the acknowledgement of service where the admission has been made or a confession statement to your affidavit. You will be asked in the affidavit to confirm that you find it intolerable to live with the respondent.

Affidavit in support of an unreasonable behaviour petition

You will be asked to confirm that the contents of your petition are true and you may supply medical evidence at this stage if you consider that the respondent's behaviour has affected your health. For example, you may exhibit to the affidavit a medical report or letter from your doctor.

Affidavit in support of a petition based on desertion

You will be asked to confirm that the contents of your petition are true, that you did not consent to the separation, and that your spouse did not offer to return to the marriage.

Affidavit in support of a petition based on two years' separation

You must confirm that you have lived separate and apart for the period of two years giving the date of separation and the addresses where you and your spouse have lived throughout that period. You must also state the date on which you reached the conclusion that your marriage was at an end, explaining the circumstances at that time.

It is possible for a husband and wife to continue living under the same roof and for the court to accept this as a separation provided you do not 'care for each other domestically'. You must live as separate households each doing your own cooking, washing and other household chores. It is possible that the registrar might require further evidence to substantiate that you have lived separate and apart for a period of two years in this sort of situation.

You will exhibit to your affidavit the acknowledgement of service duly signed by the respondent confirming consent to a decree of divorce.

Affidavit in support of a petition based on five years' separation
You must confirm that the contents of your petition are true, the date on which you separated and the addresses at which you and your spouse have lived from that date.

The pronouncement of *decree nisi* and the application for *decree absolute*
You will be notified of a date for the pronouncement of *decree nisi* which takes places in open court, usually before the morning business at 10.30 am. It is not necessary for you or your spouse to attend court to hear the pronouncement of *decree nisi*.

Decree nisi is the first decree of divorce and six weeks after it is pronounced the petitioner is normally able to apply for the decree to be made absolute. *Decree absolute* is not automatic and the petitioner must actually make an application to the court for a certificate which makes *decree nisi* absolute. Once you have received this certificate you have the final decree of divorce and only then are you free to remarry.

If the petitioner refuses or fails to apply for the *decree nisi* to be made absolute, the respondent may apply three months after the first date on which the petitioner could have applied for the certificate. For example, if *decree nisi* was pronounced on 1st May, the petitioner can first apply for *decree absolute* on June 14. If the petitioner does not apply, the respondent may apply for the *decree absolute* three months from June 14. The application must be supported by an affidavit giving reasons why the application is being made by the respondent. If no application is made by either the petitioner or the respondent and a period of 12 months elapses from the date on which *decree nisi* was pronounced, the court will require an affidavit to be sworn by the applicant, when an application for *decree absolute* is eventually made, explaining the lapse of time.

A word of warning: if you have decided to remarry as soon as you have received the certificate making *decree nisi* absolute, make sure that you have the certificate in your hand before making any fixed wedding arrangements. It is not uncommon to hear of people who have booked a hotel for the reception and paid for catering, cars, and so on, only to find that there is a hitch in obtaining *decree absolute*, which results in money being wasted and much disappointment all round.

The children's appointment

On the same day as the pronouncement of *decree nisi*, it is usual for the court to fix a short, informal appointment during which a judge considers the arrangements for the children of the family. (The arrangements for the children of the family will have been detailed in the statement which you lodged at the same time as filing the petition.)

If you and your spouse have agreed on the orders for custody, care and control, and access then the judge will normally make orders in these terms at this appointment. If no agreement has been reached, then the question of custody, care and control, and access will be adjourned to be considered more fully by the court at a later date.

It is at this appointment that the judge gives a certificate that he is satisfied with the arrangements for the children of the family. If, for any reason, the judge considers he is unable to give this certificate then it is not possible for *decree absolute* to be obtained. *Decree absolute* will be withheld until the judge has given his certificate of satisfaction. A judge may give a certificate that the arrangements for the children are the 'best in the circumstances', although not wholly satisfactory.

At this appointment before the judge you will be asked to give details of the children's living arrangements, their educational plans and to explain to the judge the arrangements that you have made with your spouse for access to and maintenance for the children.

The financial application in the petition

A petition for divorce contains a section which is technically known as a prayer for ancillary relief (see Appendix C). The prayer contains a list of the types of financial relief which the petitioner can claim. In most cases, all possible financial claims are made in the petition, and they take the following forms.

Maintenance pending suit

Maintenance pending suit refers to maintenance paid by one spouse to another before *decree absolute*. It is, in effect, an interim sum of money to keep the wife and family going until a full examination can be made of each party's income and capital position. Once these are established, the court will determine the correct amount of maintenance to be paid to the spouse and children on a long-term basis.

If you and your spouse cannot agree on the amount of interim maintenance pending a final agreement and your respective solicitors cannot help in this matter then an application for maintenance pending suit can be made as soon as the petition has been filed. The applicant will file an affidavit in support of the application setting out the present situation and giving a full picture of the applicant's financial position, and whatever is known of the respondent's financial position. The respondent must provide a full affidavit of means within 14 days to enable the registrar to make a clear decision in respect of maintenance pending suit with as much information as possible before him. If the respondent fails to provide an affidavit of means, the registrar will often make a high order for maintenance pending suit with a view to forcing the respondent to disclose his financial position to the court.

An order for maintenance pending suit is an interim order and will not last beyond *decree absolute*. The order will come into effect as soon as it is made and often an order for interim periodical payments will be made for the children of the family at the same time.

Periodical payments

An order for periodical payments to a spouse and/or to a child denotes a long-term order. An order for periodical payments can be made at any time after the pronouncement of *decree nisi* but will actually commence from the *decree absolute*. Maintenance pending suit will take care of maintenance up to *decree absolute*.

Secured periodical payments order

A secured periodical payments order is rare and can be used if there is a distinct possibility that the spouse ordered to pay maintenance will not do so or has a poor life expectancy and provided there is a fund available which can be specifically secured for the payments. A secured periodical payments order can work rather in the same way as a mortgage on a house. If you stop paying the mortgage repayments, the building society or bank will come in and sell your house in order to recoup the loan made to you. Similarly, if the payer stops paying maintenance, the fund which has been specifically set aside is forfeit and can be used for the benefit of the payee.

Lump sum order

A 'lump sum' is a capital sum of money. A lump sum order will normally be made only if there are liquid assets readily available. For example, if one spouse has a deposit account containing a sum of money, there might be a chance of a lump sum order.

Property adjustment order

A property adjustment order relates to the adjustment of ownership of property belonging to the spouses. Property can cover many types of assets including houses, cars, boats, jewellery, items of furniture, stocks and shares.

The court has substantial power to make orders relating to the property of the parties. It might, for example, order the transfer of property from single to joint ownership or from joint to single ownership. It can also order the sale of property and determine the division of the proceeds of sale, or, it can order a deferrment of the sale of the property.

Here is one example of the way in which a property adjustment order might be used:

Example of lump sum and property adjustment order

Mr and Mrs Smith own a property valued at £60,000. This property is in their joint names, and it is the matrimonial home. The mortgage on the property stands at £20,000 and this is the only capital asset of the family. There are two children, aged five and seven, and it is agreed that Mrs Smith will remain living in the house with the children and that Mr Smith will transfer the property to Mrs Smith in full and final settlement of all financial claims which she may have against her husband. It is also agreed that Mrs Smith will pay to Mr Smith a lump sum of £5,000. The ownership of the property has been transferred to Mrs Smith (a property adjustment order) on payment to Mr Smith of £5,000 (a lump sum order).

Financial relief for the children

A claim for a periodical payments order, a secured periodical payments order, or a lump sum order on behalf of any children of the family is generally made in the prayer of the petition.

The claim for custody in the petition

The prayer of the petition also includes a claim on behalf of the petitioner that he or she be granted the custody of any children of the family.

If agreement has been reached between the petitioner and the respondent before the filing of the petition that there should be an order for joint custody of the children then the word 'joint' will be inserted before 'custody' in the prayer of the petition. If no discussion on the question of custody has taken place, then it is normal for the prayer to contain a claim on the part of the petitioner for custody of the children. This can sometimes cause misunderstanding on the part of the respondent and the question of the custody, care and control, and access of the children should always be discussed between the petitioner and the respondent if this is possible (and if not then between their respective solicitors) at the earliest opportunity. Parents are encouraged to agree that there should be an order for joint custody of the children, if the parents are able to communicate with each other on a civilised and friendly basis. It is important to understand the precise meaning of the terms 'custody', 'care and control', and 'access' (see Chapter 4).

Defended divorce

Fortunately, a fully defended divorce (which is a divorce in which the respondent seeks to resist the divorce taking place) is a rare beast. This is due to a number of factors, not least the expense of a defended divorce hearing and the length of time that the matter will take to come to court.

The court, on the whole, takes the view that if the marriage has broken down for one person then the marriage has irretrievably broken down, because it is not possible to carry on a marriage on your own. Defended divorces are discouraged, and parties set on that course will often be encouraged by their advisors and by the court to reach some form of compromise.

The process of a defended divorce

1 The petitioner files the petition at the local county court.
2 A copy of the petition, a copy of the statement as to arrangements for the children, and a form of acknowledgement of service is served upon the respondent who is required to return the acknowledgement of service to the court within eight days. If the respondent intends to defend the allegations made in the petition and the statement and deny that the marriage has irretrievably broken down, then the respondent will say so on this form.
3 The respondent then has a further 21 days in which to file a document known as the 'answer'. This document is a response to the allegations made in the petition and must state the respondent's denial to the allegations and his or her version of what has happened. The respondent will state, at the end of the answer, that he/she denies that the marriage has irretrievably broken down.
4 The answer is then lodged at the court and a copy of it will be sent to the petitioner who has the right to reply in a written document, if so advised.
5 The matter will be transferred to the high court which is the venue for all defended divorces.
6 In due course an application will be made to be heard by a registrar, for directions as to the progress of the rest of the

proceedings. At this appointment, the registrar will often try to seek a compromise between the parties. If this is not possible, directions regarding the amount of time for the hearing, the number of witnesses to be called, and any other evidence will be issued.
7 Witness statements may be obtained and served on the opposing party, and the matter is eventually set down to be heard over a specific number of days in the high court. Defended divorce can now also be heard in certain county courts.
8 A fully defended divorce is heard in open court which means that any member of the public and press may attend. Needless to say it is an expensive procedure, both in terms of legal and emotional costs, for a couple to have to go through lists of allegations against each other in public.

The cross petition

Frequently, a respondent will state that he or she intends to defend the allegations made in the petition (in that they will file an answer denying the allegations made) but will accept that the marriage has irretrievably broken down. The respondent will then file what is known as a 'cross petition' in which he or she will allege, for example, that the marriage has broken down due to the behaviour, not of the respondent, but of the petitioner. Often, a petition or cross petition can be compromised, either by one party accepting that a decree can be obtained upon the other party's petition or cross petition, or by both parties obtaining decrees against each other. Frequently, honour is felt to be preserved by the latter alternative.

Hitches and hurdles

Even in this age of speedy communication, the so-called 'quickie divorce' can turn out to be a lengthy process. Take, for example, the question of custody of the children. All being well, and provided that you are in agreement with your spouse as to the orders for custody, care and control, and access, these will be dealt with at the time of the pronouncement of *decree nisi*. However, if there have been problems along the way over these issues, the whole procedure could take much longer.

Consider, too, the financial arrangements which run alongside a divorce petition. Again, if all financial issues are fully agreed between you before the pronouncement of *decree nisi*, your solicitors will detail that agreement in a document called a 'minute of order'. The document will be signed by your solicitors and lodged at the court on or any time after the pronouncement of *decree nisi* together with a statement setting out your respective financial positions. The court, if it approves the financial information and the document detailing the agreement, will make an order in those terms. But if financial issues are still in debate at the time of the pronouncement of *decree nisi*, the procedure may be held up until the problems are resolved.

So, the more you and your spouse can agree on all issues concerning finance, children and so on, before the pronouncement of *decree nisi*, then the quicker all aspects of your divorce can be dealt with. It may even be completed within the four- to five-month periods. However, if you cannot agree on certain points, divorce may take a considerable time to complete.

Judicial separation

The facts on which a decree of judicial separation is based are the same as these required for a divorce but here the similarities end. In a case of judicial separation, only one decree is granted and the parties remain legally married, although separated, after the decree has been pronounced. The court has the same powers to make financial orders that it has in proceedings for divorce.

Judicial separation proceedings are not ordinarily used these days, except where a married couple do not wish to divorce for religious reasons, or where the couple are of an age where widow's pension rights would be lost if the woman were divorced and this is an important material factor which cannot be resolved in any other way.

Deed of separation

A deed of separation is used for couples who wish to separate, or who have separated but either do not have grounds for obtaining a divorce at that time or, for some reason, do not wish to enter into divorce proceedings immediately. It is often used for couples who wish to use the two-year separation ground for divorce and who want to make definite financial arrangements pending the commencement of divorce proceedings after the two-year separation period has expired.

A deed of separation does not involve a court proceeding and therefore the deed will work only if both parties agree its terms. If you are arranging the agreement yourselves, you would be well advised each to consult a solicitor who will ensure that everything is in order and formalise the deed of separation. The deed can cover maintenance payments to a spouse and it will also deal with the distribution of family capital. Maintenance paid to a spouse under a deed of separation will enable the payer to obtain tax relief on those payments. However, maintenance paid to a child under a deed of separation will not be effective for tax relief and it is necessary that children's maintenance is dealt with under a court order. For a full explanation of the tax implications of a deed of separation, see Chapter 6.

Deed of separation or divorce

English law does not, at present, have a 'no fault' divorce proceeding for the first two years of separation. Therefore, unless either party has committed adultery or the parties have already lived 'separate and apart' for a period of two years, there is only one course open to them – that is, to make an accusation of unreasonable behaviour as reason for the breakdown of the marriage. The unreasonable behaviour petition is not pleasant, as you can imagine. One party is compelled to make allegations against the other and this rarely makes for amicable agreement on all the other issues between the parties. A couple who are left with this option alone for obtaining a divorce may wish to use a second opinion, a deed of separation pending the filing of divorce proceedings at a later date. It will detail the financial agreement reached between them, and incorporate details of any maintenance due to be paid to the wife and details of the distribution of the family capital. It is also possible to insert a clause to state that when the parties have been separated for a period of two years, one of them will petition for a divorce on the basis that they have then lived 'separate and apart' for a continuous period of two years, and that the other party consents to divorce proceedings.

If you wish to use a deed of separation in order to confirm and complete the financial arrangements between you both, then you must make a full disclosure to one another of your true financial position. This is one of the reasons why it is wise to consult a solicitor; he or she will check that you have complied with all necessary steps in order to render your deed of separation valid and enforceable.

If, when you eventually go through divorce proceedings, you intend to ask the court to confirm the financial arrangement reached between you and your spouse when drawing up the deed of separation and make it the final financial arrangement, it is essential that there has been a full disclosure of your respective financial positions. Without this, the court may well consider the deed of separation to be an interim measure and decide that the financial issue should be looked at and determined afresh. (See Appendix D for an example of a deed of separation.)

Chapter 3

How to handle your own divorce proceedings

It is important to remember that divorce proceedings themselves will deal with all the aspects of the family on divorce:

(a) The proceedings for the divorce leading to a decree of divorce;
(b) Agreement or dispute as to custody and access;
(c) Agreement or proceedings relating to the financial issues.

Each of these three aspects can be agreed upon before the proceedings for divorce are commenced, thus ensuring that the agreement with regard to the arrangements for the children and the financial agreement can both be dealt with in court orders shortly after the pronouncement of *decree nisi*.

If no agreement can be reached with regard either to the custody of or access to the children, this will have to be dealt with at a later date by the court. Similarly, if no agreement can be reached on a suitable financial settlement this will also have to be dealt with by the court at a later date (see Chapter 6).

If agreement has been reached between you and your spouse on all issues and you have checked those agreements with a solicitor, there is no reason why you should not deal with the mechanics of the legal proceedings yourself. Every county court with divorce jurisdiction will be able to supply you with the appropriate forms and explanation of the procedure. If you live in central London the forms are available from the Divorce Registry.

The procedure

1 Approach the court office of your local county court explaining that you wish to handle your own divorce proceedings. Some county courts actually provide a 'do-it-yourself pack'. If you file

the petition, you will be known as the petitioner, while your spouse will be known as the respondent.

2 Complete:
   (a) A form of petition for divorce (see Appendix C);
   (b) A statement of arrangements for the children, if there are children of the marriage (see Appendix C).

3 Lodge with these forms the original or a certified copy (not an ordinary photocopy) of your marriage certificate (a certified copy can be obtained from the Registry of Births, Marriages & Deaths).

4 Lodge a petition fee of £40 unless you are exempt by virtue of your income level (see Chapter 9).

5 Copies of the petition (and statement of arrangements for the children) will be sent to your spouse together with a form of acknowledgement of service (see Appendix C). Service of the petition personally by you the petitioner is not acceptable to the court so make sure that service of the petition is done by post by the court.

6 Your spouse will complete the form of acknowledgement of service and send it back to the court.

7 The court will stamp the form of acknowledgement of service and will send a photocopy to you, the petitioner.

8 Obtain from the court office, if you have not already done so, an affidavit in support of your petition. (Appendix C gives an example of an affidavit in support of a two-year separation petition.) Complete this and attach to it a copy of the acknowledgement of service duly signed by the respondent. The affidavit must be 'sworn' either before a solicitor who will make a charge of £3.75 or at the court office where there is no charge.

9 The affidavit is then lodged at the court together with a form of request for directions for trial. In due course it will come before a registrar who will ensure that the correct procedure has been adhered to and that the grounds for divorce and basis of the petition have been proved. You will then be notified of a date for the pronouncement of *decree nisi*.

10 It is not necessary for you to attend court for the pronouncement of *decree nisi*. A certificate of *decree nisi* will be sent to you and to your spouse in due course.

11 Six weeks after the pronouncement of *decree nisi* you, as petitioner, can complete the appropriate form. Lodge it at the court and a certificate making *decree nisi* absolute will be sent to you within a few days. There is a fee of £10 payable on the application for a certificate making *decree nisi* absolute. The certificate is the document you will need if you wish to remarry. Keep the certificate in a

safe place, as you will have to present the original to the Registrar of Marriages on remarriage and it is difficult to obtain a duplicate.

Children

If there are children in your family and agreement has been reached between you and your spouse as to the orders for custody and access (see Chapter 4) then the court will be able to make these orders when you and your spouse attend a short informal appointment before the judge. This 10-minute appointment is held to allow the judge time to consider the arrangements for the children. The court must be satisfied with the arrangements made for the children's accommodation, maintenance, education and so on before it will allow the *decree nisi* to be made absolute.

If the judge is satisfied he will give a certificate of satisfaction and the application for *decree absolute* can go ahead six weeks later. If the judge for any reason declines to give his certificate, after the date upon which the *decree nisi* was pronounced, no application can be made for the final decree and you would probably be wise to consult a solicitor at this point.

It is at this appointment that the judge will make orders for the custody, care and control, and access to the children if these matters have been agreed between you. Your solicitor may or may not accompany you to this appointment.

Finance

If you have reached agreement with your spouse on a division of the family finances, you may ask the court at any time after the pronouncement of *decree nisi* to incorporate that agreement into a final financial order within the divorce proceedings. You would be wise to seek legal advice on the agreement at this stage and to ask your solicitor to draft the agreement into a document suitable for the court, if you have not already done so. The registrar of the court is very likely to ask you both to attend a meeting so that he can speak to you about the agreement. You will also be asked to complete a form (Rule 76A Form) which is a statement giving the following information:

(a) The duration of the marriage;
(b) The age of each spouse and the age of any minor children of the family;
(c) An estimate of the amount of capital of each spouse and any minor child;

(d) The net income of each spouse and any minor child of the family;
(e) Details of the arrangements for the accommodation of each spouse and any minor child of the family;
(f) Whether either spouse has remarried or has any present intention of remarriage or co-habitation with another person;
(g) Where the order provides for a transfer of property, confirmation that any mortgagee of that property has been served with notice of the application and that within 14 days of service no objection has been made to the transfer;
(h) Any other specifically relevant matters.

If the registrar is satisfied that each spouse has disclosed their true financial position to the other and that, in the circumstances, the financial agreement appears fair and just, he will make an order in those terms and a sealed copy of the order will be sent to you and your spouse in due course.

Generally, it will be possible for you to handle the financial side of your divorce proceedings only if you believe your spouse to be open and honest with you. Even if this is the case, it is sensible to check any financial agreement with a solicitor. One hour spent with a solicitor taking basic advice and checking any agreement may save you much time, heartache and legal costs in the future.

Most people who deal with their own divorce proceedings tend to be young couples with no children where each party has an income and there is little or no property. In this sort of case only the mechanics of obtaining a decree of divorce are relevant and the couple may handle the process following the guidelines above.

Chapter 4

Looking after the children

One issue which often raises the temperature in divorce proceedings is the question of the custody of the children. One method of ensuring that you both approach the discussions as calmly as possible is by finding out exactly what the terms custody, care and control, and access actually mean. You should know, too, that the legal custody of legitimate children vests jointly in the parents unless, and until, an order is made to the contrary by the court.

Conciliation

The concept of conciliation is one which is growing rapidly in family law. The purpose of conciliation is to help couples to find an acceptable solution to the problems they face. Conciliation at present tends to be used only where there is a dispute over the custody, care and control or access to the children although moves are afoot to enlarge the scope of conciliation within family law.

There are a number of family conciliation services throughout the country. It is the function of these services to provide an experienced and trained professional who is independent of the parties and their solicitors and who will provide the environment in which couples can discuss, with the help of the conciliator, the problems which they are encountering. Conciliation allows both spouses to express their views and possibly to reach an agreement acceptable to both, without the pressure which the adversarial approach of a contested hearing inevitably produces.

Many Family Conciliation Services are affiliated to the National Family Conciliation Council. You will find your nearest service by contacting the NFCC at 34 Milton Road, Swindon, Wiltshire SN1 5JA (please send SAE) or your local Citizen's Advice Bureau will provide you with information on your local service.

Many courts in England and Wales now have an 'in court' conciliation scheme where a registrar with the help of a conciliator, usually a court welfare officer, will attempt to help couples to reach a decision over disputes which have arisen over the children. The 'in court' scheme is discussed below.

Joint custody

If as parents you are able to communicate on a civilised, if not amicable, basis about your children, and you both agree to continue sharing the parenting of your children then the option you are likely to choose is joint custody.

Joint custody gives both parents the right to take part in the major decisions in a child's life. These are – generally speaking – deciding on the child's education, religious upbringing and medical care. For example, do you wish your son or daughter to be educated in the state or the private sector? Joint custody gives both parents the right to discuss this issue and to take a joint decision. With regard to religious education, again, joint custody gives each parent the right to have a say in the matter. Clearly, if the parents cannot agree on a religion for the child, then the matter must ultimately be dealt with by the court – whether or not there is an order for joint or sole custody. The major issue concerning medical care is generally based on consent to medical treatment.

Fortunately, a large number of parents accept the fact that although they are unable to live together as husband and wife, this does not mean that they cannot continue to be parents to their children. Many couples are able to organise and share this on a civilised basis, which is obviously the most desirable option for parents and children. An order for joint custody is a tremendous help for the children particularly, because it shows them that although their parents have decided to separate and perhaps to divorce, the disagreements are between the parents in their roles as husband and wife rather than as father and mother. The children often feel more stable with a joint custody order because it helps them to realise that their parents are still equally interested in their welfare and upbringing.

Sole custody

Statistically there are more sole orders made than orders for joint custody. Parents are being encouraged more and more to try and agree sufficiently over the children to make a joint custody order viable.

Where a sole custody order is granted, for example to the mother, it allows her to make decisions with regard to the child and specifically those which relate to education, religion and medical care. The sole custody order does not wholly exclude the other parent in that there is a duty on the custodial parent to keep the non-custodian informed as to the children's welfare, activities, educational and religious plans. Also, it is possible for the non-custodial parent to have access to the child or children. He or she will, therefore, have direct contact with them and be able to keep in touch with the events in their lives.

The non-custodial parent can make an application to the court for directions without seeking to vary the custody order, if he or she feels that the custodial parent is not acting in the child's best interest especially over religious and educational matters.

A sole custody order is often granted in a situation where the parents have experienced a particularly acrimonious separation and divorce and as a result are quite unable to communicate with each other. If for this, or for any other reason, their communication simply results in angry abuse, then it may be considered impossible for the parents to discuss rationally the plans for their children's future. In these cases, the sole custody order might very well be granted.

Care and control

There is in principle complete equality between parents with regard to the care and control of the children. However, in practice the care and control of the children normally goes to the parent with whom the children are living or are going to be living. The parent with care and control will be responsible for the day-to-day care of the children. It would be unheard of these days for an order for sole custody to be awarded to the father, and an order for care and control to the mother. This, quite clearly, could cause the most enormous problems.

If there is an order for joint custody and the parent with care and control dies, the surviving parent will normally assume care and control of the children. If there is an order for sole custody and the parent with sole custody dies, the non-custodial parent can apply to the court for custody, care and control.

Who will have the care and control of the children – mother or father?

There are no set rules but generally a mother will be granted care and control of young children. In a family where the mother has stopped work to look after the children from birth or perhaps works part-time, it would be usual for the children to continue living with their mother and to have access to their father who could continue with his career and supply finance for the family.

The court is normally reluctant to separate children from the same family unless there are special circumstances or unless the parents agree.

Older children, especially older male children may wish to live with their father. Unless there are serious reasons why a 15-year-old boy, for example, should not live with his father, then the court will generally grant that request. However, it is still quite difficult for a father to obtain care and control of the children, especially young children. The father must prove to the court that the mother is unable to care for the children properly, perhaps because of mental instability or some other serious factor. The father must also prove to the court that he has suitable accommodation for the child and has made arrangements for its day-to-day care in the event that he is unable to do this himself.

Ultimately any dispute between parents over care and control of the children must be resolved by the court.

Access

The term used by the court when awarding access is 'reasonable access'. On the whole, the courts do not wish to define access too specifically, believing that it is unwise to restrict the parents and children to a rigid pattern. By leaving the order as reasonable access, the parents are free to work out a plan which suits both themselves and the children. This helps considerably as children grow older and become involved in their own activities such as brownies, cubs, sports, music and socialising with their own friends. Once this begins, a rigid pattern of access, which demands that the child be in a certain place at a certain time with a certain parent, could hardly benefit the child. At times like this, it is important to remember that it is the child's right to have access to the parent just as much as it is the parent's right to have access to the child.

How much access?

Frequency of access varies from family to family. The arrangements made regarding how often the non-custodial parent may see his or her offspring will also differ. It may depend on the distance between the separated parents, their working hours or numerous other factors. As a rough guide, parents who live a reasonable distance from each other and who have a reasonable relationship might organise a pattern of access along the following lines. Staying access might stretch from Friday evening through to Sunday evening or perhaps from Saturday morning through to Sunday evening. This might take place on alternate weekends, although sometimes parents prefer staying access to be one weekend in three.

Sometimes, parents agree to share every school holiday equally.

Alternatively, if one parent has a limited amount of annual holiday, say four weeks a year, agreements are often made which allow this parent to spend, for example, two weeks during the summer holidays, one week at Easter, one week at Christmas, and part of each half term with the child or children. Over Christmas and Easter, it is quite usual for parents to agree, for example, that one parent has the children for Christmas and the other has them for New Year one year, then vice versa the next year. This system can be applied to any other religious festival.

Calm and considered discussion with your spouse about the frequency and pattern of access to the children will help enormously when it comes to final decision-making. The question of access can raise any number of difficulties, especially during the very emotional and difficult period when the parties first separate or when they decide to institute divorce proceedings. Whatever the pair of you feel about each other and about your present situation, and despite the insecurity that you may be experiencing, make sure that your children do not take the brunt of the suffering. It is not their fault that your marriage is going through these difficulties and too often they are treated like just another chattel to be used for bargaining purposes. Children understand a great deal, far more than adults think, so do not imagine that the difficulties between you and your spouse go unnoticed. It is probably best to discuss the situation with them openly and calmly. Explain to them in simple terms exactly what is going on and make sure that they understand that they are not to blame for the break-up of the marriage. Above all, remember that the children, too, need constant comfort and reassurance that their own security is not being jeopardised.

Once a pattern of access has been agreed, the children may be moody, irritable and generally difficult on their return home from an access visit. This is quite normal, and does not necessarily mean that the children do not wish to visit that parent again, or that they have been ill-treated in any way or do not want to return to the parent with whom they are living. If their irritability and unsettled feelings are dealt with calmly and thoughtfully, the children generally relax into the routine you have worked out, and feelings of torn loyalty will probably diminish.

Travelling abroad with the children

Every custody order made in any court in England and Wales will state that the child is not to be removed from the jurisdiction (ie England and Wales) without the consent of the other parent, or leave of the court, until he or she is 18 years old. A parent planning to travel abroad with the children on holiday must lodge a general undertaking with the court to return the children to England and Wales if and when called upon to do so. (This does not have to be done every time you leave the country, merely the first time.) In the event that one parent (irrespective of his or her custodial status) still refuses consent to the children leaving the jurisdiction, an application must be made to the court for leave to take the children out of the jurisdiction for the duration of the holiday. This sort of application will normally be granted, unless the court considers that there is a sufficient risk that the parent taking the children abroad would not return them and, in fact, intends to stay abroad permanently.

In some cases, the court will ask the parent concerned to lodge a bond with the court. A bond consists of a sum of money which would be forfeited if the children were not returned on time. Sometimes, the money can be used by the remaining parent to cover legal costs and travel expenses in securing the return of the children.

Change of name

An order granting custody or care and control to a parent states that that parent may not take any steps to change the child's surname without the consent of the other parent or an order of the court. The court in considering such an application will give consideration as to whether it is in the interest of the child for his or her surname to be changed.

Disputes over custody, care and control, and access

Unfortunately, it is not uncommon for there to be disagreement between parents over the way in which custody, care and control, and access is to be organised. Many people find themselves in a custody dispute because one party is 'holding out' for custody of the children. One of the reasons this occurs so frequently is because the true nature of custody, care and control and access has not be explained properly. They may fear that they will lose touch completely with their children if they are denied sole custody. A custody dispute is to be avoided if at all possible. it causes severe emotional trauma not only to the parents but also to the children who are generally well aware that their parents are fighting over them. It is also an expensive activity even if you are able to obtain legal aid (Chapter 9). A custody dispute is often a most unpleasant experience for everyone concerned, especially as other members of the family such as grandparents, aunts and uncles are required to be involved.

Before you embark on a formal dispute over custody, make sure that you have fully considered whether or not this course of action is in the best interest of your children.

In a number of divorce courts, the question of a custody dispute can be dealt with via the in-court conciliation procedure. This procedure enables parents to discuss, with the help of a third party (usually a court welfare officer) the problems they are encountering over the question of custody, care and control and access. Any emotional problems that the parents experience with the children as a result of the breakdown of the marriage may also be discussed. The conciliation procedure gives the parents the opportunity to discuss their fears and opposition to custody and/or access. The procedure provides a third party, skilled in conciliation, who works with the parents to help them reach a workable agreement between themselves.

In any dispute over who should have the custody, and care and control of the children where the initial conciliation procedure has failed to achieve an agreement, both parents will have to follow the recognised court procedures.

1 The parent who seeks custody, and care and control of the children will make the application to the court supported by an affidavit giving his or her reasons why the other party should not be entitled to a joint custody order. This affidavit will invite a reply from the other parent.
2 A court welfare officer will be appointed to discuss matters fully with each parent, and with the children if they are of an age to express any opinion. Eventually, the court welfare officer will prepare a report having considered any other factors which may be relevant to the case. These might include, for example, the role of a grandparent in the children's upbringing, comments from teachers, and opinions from doctors. This information is in the form of a written report because, on the whole, the court does not welcome a string of witnesses for both parties each proclaiming the virtues of the specific parent. However, in addition to the court welfare officer's report, the court occasionally requires evidence from the children's teacher, social worker or doctor, in which case this person will usually be asked to give evidence in court.
3 Once all this material has been gathered, the matter will be set down for a hearing before a judge. At the end of that hearing the judgement will be given, and an order made as to the custody and care and control of the children.

The court system in the United Kingdom is an adversarial system and as such is thought by many family law solicitors to be an unfortunate forum for a dispute between two parents about their children. It is, by nature, accusatorial and in a situation where emotions are already heightened, the system does little to encourage conciliation. The priority here should be to provide a situation where the parents themselves can agree on the future of their children – if on nothing else.

Disputes over access

A dispute over access to the children is probably more common than a dispute over custody. When there are signs of a serious and growing dispute over access, it is often a good step to approach your local conciliation service for help. Conciliation services have been established in many areas to help parents understand and resolve their own emotional difficulties over access to their children. It is a forum in which parents can meet and discuss their difficulties with the help of a third party. The third person will be prepared either to join in a discussion between you and your spouse, or to meet each of you separately in an attempt to resolve the situation in that way. This service enables many parents to find a solution to the problem themselves without the need of court proceedings. As noted above, many courts have introduced a conciliation proceeding within the court procedure.

In-court conciliation procedure

The in-court conciliation procedure is one of the methods used to try and help parents resolve their inability to come to an agreement over custody and access arrangements. In circumstances where the solicitors themselves have been unable to help the parties resolve the dispute or in circumstances where there is no out-of-court conciliation service, or no agreement could be reached with the help of that service, an application will be made to the court for access to be defined. This application, instead of entering the normal process of the adversarial system, will enter the conciliation scheme.

1 An appointment will be given to you with a registrar and a court welfare officer. Both parents will be expected to attend with their solicitors and, certainly as far as the divorce registrars in central London are concerned, all children over the age of nine years old to whom the dispute relates will also be expected to attend the court on that day. The children themselves do not enter the courtroom at all. On arrival, they are taken to a waiting room where they may chat to the court welfare officer about their feelings on access, if it is felt necessary to ask them.

2 At the conciliation appointment, the parties' solicitors will explain to the registrar the basis of the problem. Once this has been established, the court welfare officer will take both parties from the room and speak to them either together or separately, depending

on the way that particular court welfare officer deals with the procedure.
3 He or she will generally speak to the children if they are present.

At the beginning of the appointment, the registrar should explain to the couple that anything said at the appointment or to the court welfare officer is said in confidence and, should conciliation fail, cannot be used in evidence or in an affidavit in subsequent contentious proceedings. For example, it would be quite wrong to state in a subsequent affidavit: 'She told the welfare officer at the conciliation appointment that she would let me have access to the children just so long as my girlfriend wasn't present.'

The conciliation appointment and its confidentiality is designed to encourage the couple to talk out the problems and to try and find a solution without feeling constrained by the legal procedures and nervous about what they should or should not be saying.

If the conciliation procedure fails and no agreement can be reached, the matter will proceed into the adversarial system and both parties will be asked to file affidavit evidence setting out their case, as described above.

The in-court conciliation procedures are, in many areas, still in their infancy and there is always room for improvement. In fact, many practitioners are monitoring the services in their areas and suggesting positive changes.

Out-of-court conciliation

The number of out-of-court conciliation services being established is increasing all the time. Some are good and, inevitably some are not so good. The National Family Conciliation Council (see Appendix A) provides a list of out-of-court conciliation services throughout England and Wales (see Appendix E). Your local conciliation service is there to help you. You do not have to have a solicitor before approaching the service and you can go to them with any problem whatsoever relating to custody or access, at any time. It is always worth consulting your local conciliation service even before you make an appointment with a solicitor.

Child abduction

When a parent removes a child or children from the other parent without his or her consent, whatever the state of the marriage and whatever the agreement for custody, it may be considered to be a case of child abduction. The number of incidents of child abduction has increased in recent years. The sophistication of life throughout the world and the increase in travel between countries has lead to a rise in the number of mixed nationality marriages and also a rise in the number of disputes between parents as to the custody and residence of their children after a breakdown of the marriage. Many people these days seem to have friends, if not relatives, who live abroad. If your spouse has relatives or easy access to another country and you feel that he or she is likely to take the children and 'disappear', then you should contact a solicitor immediately. A set procedure exists within the family jurisdiction designed specifically to stop the removal of children from England and Wales without both parents' consent.

The wardship procedure

If you have a strong belief that your spouse has an intention of removing your child or children from England and Wales, that is to say the jurisdiction of the English court, and you have some evidence to support that belief, you should contact a solicitor as a matter of urgency and consideration will be given as to whether the child should be made a Ward of Court.

If there is evidence that your spouse has plans to remove the child, your solicitor will make an application to the court, making the child a ward of the English court. This means that the court in theory will have the custody of the child during the wardship and the court must be consulted on all matters relating to the child during that period. An appointment with a registrar of the court will be made within 21 days of the application and your spouse will be served with the papers informing him or her that the child is not to be removed from the jurisdiction. At that appointment, it is usual that a Court Welfare Officer will be appointed to report to the court on the issues between you over custody, care and control, and access and a date set for a hearing of the matter before a judge for a decision to be made. The Court Welfare Officer will interview both spouses and the child, if appropriate, and any other person he or she considers relevant, before preparing the report for the court.

If matters have taken a more serious turn and, for example, the children are already with your spouse and may have already left the country an application should be made at the first available opportunity:
1 To make the child a Ward of Court;
2 To obtain what is known as a 'seek and find' order;
3 To apply for a 'bench warrant' to be attached to that order.

On the making of a seek and find order a court official known as the Tipstaff will be called in and it is his job to take all reasonable steps to locate the child. Interpol will be informed and usually the press are called in to help. If a bench warrant is attached to that order, the Tipstaff is given power by the court to arrest the 'abducting spouse' and to bring that spouse before the court at the earliest opportunity.

The procedure usually works effectively if the children have not already left the jurisdiction. If they have already left, difficulties do arise in securing their return through the process of law in a foreign country, although the Child Abduction and Custody Act 1985 (see below) does provide a mechanism to the parent but only if the child is in a country which has ratified the relevant conventions.

If you find yourself in a position of having to make an application to the court you should take with you a recent photograph of the children and give as much information to the Tipstaff as possible about details such as what they were wearing. If you have the childrens' birth certificates you should hand these to your solicitor. Emergency legal aid is available for an application to make a child a ward of court. (For emergency legal aid see Chapter 9.)

The removal of a child from England and Wales to, for example, a Muslim country may make it almost impossible to secure his or her return without the agreement of the removing parent, due to the nature of the law in such countries.

Muslim law provides its own rules as to the custody of a child in divorce. It is usual for the custody of a boy child of five years and over to be granted automatically to the father and the custody of a girl child to the father at puberty. A Muslim divorce is called a Talaq and is effective by the husband pronouncing 'I divorce you' three times. The divorce must then be registered in a Muslim court. A woman has no right of audience in a Muslim court and no right to be heard on the question of divorce. Therefore if a child has been abducted and taken to a Muslim country by the father, a mother's ability to put her case for custody in that court is most unlikely to be successful if opposed by the father.

From 2 May 1986, the police in England and Wales have provided 24-hour cover to alert all ports and airports and points of exit from England and Wales using a national computer to link them with immigration officers. Before that date, the 'all ports alert' for children at risk was dealt with by the Home Office. When there is a real threat that a child is about to be removed unlawfully from England and Wales all ports will be informed directly by the police. It is not now necessary to obtain a court order in respect of a child under 16 before you seek police assistance. If, however, you have obtained an order you should show this to the police. If your child has been abducted or you believe your child to have been abducted, first inform the police and then contact a solicitor and consider making that child a ward of court.

Before the police institute a port-alert they will need to be satisfied that the danger of the removal of the child from the jurisdiction is real and imminent. 'Imminent' means within 24 or 48 hours and 'real' means that the port-alert is not being sought by, or on behalf of, the applicant merely as an insurance. If the police decide the situation is such that a port-alert should be used, the child's name will remain on the stop list for four weeks. After that time the child's name will be removed automatically from the stop list unless a further application is made.

It is advisable to consider giving notice in writing to the passport office if you believe that there is a chance your child may be removed from the jurisdiction. Your request should be that all passport facilities should be refused in respect of the child.

The idea of abducting your children may, at times, seem like the only answer to your problems over gaining access to them, but it really is not. Before you go any further, think carefully about the experience of abduction from a child's point of view. It is always a selfish move, and one which inevitably leads to long-term problems for you and the rest of your family. In addition, it may severely curtail your rights to access and to joint custody of your children.

The Child Abduction Act (1984) makes it a criminal offence to remove a child under the age of 16 years from England and Wales without the consent of his or her parent or guardian or leave of the court if the child is subject to a custody order or is a ward of court. The offence of abduction carries a prison sentence.

Taking action once the children are abroad

The United Kingdom has now passed into law the Child Abduction and Custody Act (1985) which ratified parts of the Hague Convention of 1980 and The European Convention of 1980. The Act has increased the chance of the return of a child who has been removed from the jurisdiction in that, if a child under the age of 16 years is taken to a country which has ratified the conventions (see below) without the consent of its parent, the court of the foreign country, if there is no current custody order, must order the return of that child to the country from whence it came for the question of custody to be determined. Your spouse can therefore be ordered by a foreign country to return the child immediately.

If there is a current custody order and the child has been removed abroad to one of the member countries, the foreign court has power to enforce that custody order made under the country of the child's nationality and thus order its return.

The Child Abduction and Custody Act 1985 is administered by the Lord Chancellor's Department which has stated that legal aid will be given to applicants under the act, irrespective of their means, in order to facilitate litigation in a foreign country for the return of an abducted child or for the enforcement of a custody decision.

Once the return of the child has been secured and if no agreement as to the future can be reached, the matter must be dealt with by the court.

The Children's Legal Centre has produced an information sheet entitled Child Abduction which provides a checklist of what to do if a child is abducted, and the precautions which can be taken if an abduction is imminent. This information sheet can be obtained from 20 Compton Terrace, London N1 2UN. The Children Abroad Self-Help Group, Keighley Gingerbread Advice Centre, 33 Barlow Road, Keighley, West Yorkshire also offers help and advice for parents of children who have been abducted. The membership fee is £15.

Chapter 5

Violence – protection for the family

You may think that you would never resort to violence against your spouse however bad your situation becomes and that, similarly, your spouse would never resort to violence against you. If you are proved wrong, don't be too surprised. The breakdown of a relationship and marriage is a tense and emotional time and many strong feelings are to the fore. In a situation where a marriage is deteriorating and the parties are still living under the same roof, tensions will increase and tempers may be raised. It is often under these circumstances that violence occurs. It is not uncommon to hear people who have used physical violence against their partners explaining that they are unable to understand why they resorted to violence because it is not in their nature. When feelings run high, some people find themselves reduced to their last resource, which is usually physical strength.

Taking action against violence

Sadly, there are many relationships in which one spouse suffers violence from the other on a regular basis. If your spouse uses physical violence against you, try to get away from the place in which it happens as soon as possible. If you are at home and feel frightened that by remaining there you might be injured further, leave at once. If there are children in the house try to take them with you. If this is difficult, work out how safe it is for them to remain. If your spouse has been violent to the children in the past, it would be wise to take them with you at all costs.

The next step is to telephone the police and explain what has happened. This sort of incident qualifies as an emergency and therefore you are entitled to dial 999. Many people think that the police are unwilling to interfere in domestic disputes. In fact they are prepared to give immediate assistance and will try to calm the situation. They will probably also advise you to seek help from a solicitor as soon as possible. If you are a woman (with or without children) in need of somewhere to stay for the night, ask the police to give you the telephone number and address of the local women's refuge. Alternatively, if you are unable to return to your home, telephone your local authority's emergency housing department and explain your predicament to them. If you have been injured in any way by the violence, go directly to your doctor, or to the casualty department of the nearest hospital for treatment. If you are unable to leave the house, try to protect yourself by moving as far away as possible from your spouse and try to calm the situation. Contact your solicitor as soon as you can. If you do not have a solicitor, the Citizen's Advice Bureau or your local police station will be able to suggest one.

If you have been forced to leave your children behind, you should telephone the police immediately and tell them that you have done so. If possible, you should also telephone the local social services department and explain what has happened. Don't imagine that by leaving the children, for some reason or another you will lose the children for good. You do not lose you rights as a parent if you are forced to leave your children because of violence by your spouse. However, it is important to take immediate action to have them returned to you.

Contact a solicitor as soon as you can

When you meet your solicitor, he or she will take a statement from you in which you explain exactly what happened, and will then assess whether or not it is possible to make an application to the court for an injunction (provisional order of the court) restraining your spouse from being violent towards you and the children.

Some injunctions carry a power of arrest which means that if the injunction is disobeyed the police, if they are called, have the power to arrest your spouse. If the police are unable to enforce the court order, because there is no power of arrest attached to the injunction then you must return to the court where the judge will consider committal to prison for breach of a court order.

Obtaining an injunction

The court has power to make injunctions and orders for the protection of spouses and children. Those orders and injunctions fall into two categories:

A non-molestation injunction. This restrains your spouse from assaulting, molesting or otherwise interfering with you and/or the children.

An ouster injunction. This order excludes a spouse from the house or restricts the use of the house to specified areas.

In the magistrates court a non-molestation injunction is known as a protection order and an ouster injunction as an exclusion order.

An application for protection from violence can be made as follows:
1 Within divorce proceedings in the county court;
2 In the magistrates court under the Domestic Proceedings and Magistrates Courts Act 1978;
3 In the county court under the Domestic Violence Act 1978. (This Act is also open to cohabitees who suffer violence.)

An order excluding a spouse from the house or restricting use can be made as follows:
1 Under the Matrimonial Homes Act in the county court;
2 Under the Domestic Proceedings and Magistrates Court Act 1978 in the magistrates court.

An injunction is an emergency procedure which will not be used unless you are able to convince the court both that violence has occurred, and that you are fearful that it will happen again unless an injunction is made and served upon your spouse. This explains why the application must be made to the court as soon as it is reasonably possible after the incidence of violence. If you delay taking action for a while, your fear that the violence might recur will be less convincing. The violence must also be considered 'sufficient' to warrant applying for an injunction. There are no strict guidelines specifying degrees of violence and the solicitor will use his or her judgement and experience.

Recent case law has made it more difficult for one party to oust the other party from the family home by way of court order. As a compromise, the court might make an order demanding that the parties each keep to different parts of the house. If this happens, the court will define the area which each spouse may occupy under the injunction.

This sort of injunction is usually seen as a provisional measure prior to a final order in financial proceedings within divorce proceedings. Once the final financial order is made, the future of both spouses and any children of the family can be determined and organised on a permanent basis. It is possible for injunction proceedings to be taken *ex parte* (this means without the knowledge of the spouse against whom the violence is alleged). If the court considers the violence to be such as to be necessary to grant an injunction, a copy of the injunction will be served upon the defendant (ie the person against whom the allegations of violence are made) together with a notice of the date on which the matter is to be returned to the court. Usually, injunction proceedings are dealt with fairly quickly, so the return date will normally be within a week or so. Return dates are not always given. The reason the judge gives a return date is to allow the defendant to come to court and to put his or her side of the story. It is at this second hearing that the judge decides whether or not the injunction should be continued and, if it is not to be continued, whether certain undertakings are required from either party.

If you are the recipient of an injunction together with a notice giving you a return date, contact a solicitor as soon as possible. The solicitor will take a statement from which he or she will then turn into an affidavit.

Sometimes when the parties attend the court on the return date a compromise is reached outside the door of the court, usually through their solicitors. The defendant might agree to offer an undertaking to the court that he or she will refrain from assaulting, molesting or otherwise interfering with the other spouse and/or the children of the family. The undertaking is regarded as a promise to the court and if the promise is broken, the defendant can expect to be treated as if he or she had broken a court order. Breach of a court order is contempt of court and can lead to a prison sentence.

The ability to obtain an injunction relates not only to a married couple but also to a man and woman who are cohabiting. In this case, proceedings will take place in your local county court under the Domestic Violence and Matrimonial Proceedings Act (1976).

Chapter 6

The financial arrangements

The financial application
The petitioner makes claims for ancillary relief (financial relief) in the prayer of the petition. In order to proceed with those claims, if no agreement has been reached between the parties, the petitioner must serve a notice of intention to proceed and lodge this, together with an affidavit of means in support of the financial application, at the court. The affidavit of means must give a full and detailed picture of the petitioner's financial position, and as much of the respondent's financial position as is known to the petitioner. A copy of the affidavit and notice of intention to proceed is served upon the respondent who has 14 days in which to serve an affidavit of means upon the petitioner in reply. In this, the respondent must set out his or her true financial position; he or she is free to comment on any statement made in the petitioner's affidavit.

The court requires a full disclosure of the true financial position from both parties. Failure to provide this can, in some circumstances, lead to the re-opening of a final financial settlement with the resulting legal expense and possible increase in the amount ordered to be paid by one party to the other. Furthermore, failure to disclose fully one's financial position can lead to delays and acrimony. As a guideline, your affidavit of means should cover the following matters.

Income
State, in your affidavit, your income from all sources:
1 Gross and net salary from employment including overtime and any benefits which you receive by virtue of your employment, for example, expense account, luncheon vouchers, car etcetera;
2 If you are self-employed, give your income for the past three years and tax and National Insurance paid;
3 Income from extra or freelance work;

58 *Divorce and Separation*

4 Payments from the DHSS such as child benefit, disability allowance or any other benefit.

Interest on any investments or accounts
1 Income from stocks and shares or any other investments;
2 Your income from Lloyds if you are a member;
3 Income from pensions, for example disability pensions, service pension.

Capital value of your property
1 Value of any property, whether in this country or abroad, which you may own;
2 Value of car(s);
3 Value of boat, caravan or any other movable property.

If you have any item of particular value in the matrimonial home, you should state this item and its value separately. For example, antique furniture, paintings, jewellery, fur coats, hi-fi equipment, silver, china, glass. Remember that the price which you paid for ordinary household goods and contents will not generally reflect the true re-sale value which will be substantially lower. The figure given by insurance companies is the replacement value of the item rather than its re-sale value.

Liabilities
(a) Amount of outstanding mortgage;
(b) Details of hire purchase agreements, loan agreements;
(c) Details of bank overdrafts;
(d) Details of outstanding balance on all credit cards;
(e) Details of balance on department store charge cards etcetera;
(f) Details of any other debts such as tax liabilities.

Outgoings and general expenditure
This list will of course differ depending on your circumstances but the following example may help to jog your memory when compiling the list for yourself or for your solicitor.

Mortgage repayments
Repayment of any other loan
Repayment of any HP agreement
Repayment of credit card account or other charge card accounts

Electricity
Gas
Telephone
Rates
Water rates
House (and contents) insurance

Other insurance, such as life insurance, private health insurance
Mortgage protection policy
Pension contribution

House repairs
Repairs to household equipment
Car repairs and services
Car insurance, tax, AA/RAC subscription

Food and household necessities
Clothing and shoes
Cosmetics and toiletries
Child minder
Cleaning person
Window cleaner
Dry cleaning
Travel fares
Lunches
School lunches
Newspapers and magazines
Pets and pet food
Christmas and birthday presents

Entertainment
Holidays
Children's activities – brownies, cubs, dancing, music lessons
Sport and sports equipment
Television licence and rental
Video rental
Subscriptions to clubs, magazines and associations
School fees

It is always more expensive to maintain two households than one and you will inevitably, in most cases, experience a drop in your standard of living on a separation or divorce. However, it is useful to provide a list along the lines of the example above so that the necessary and essential elements can be determined to establish a proper level of maintenance.

Once both parties have sworn an affidavit of means, their legal advisers may consider it necessary to request copies of various documents in order to establish the truth of the statements. It is usual for both parties' solicitors to provide each other with the documents they wish to inspect and for these documents to be available to the court at the final hearing. The documents which you may be asked to provide will include some or all of the following:

(a) A copy of bank statements on all bank accounts for the last 18 months to three years;
(b) A copy of credit card statements on all credit card accounts for the last 18 months to three years;
(c) A copy of department store charge accounts;
(d) A copy of electricity, gas, and telephone accounts;
(e) A copy of your payslip;
(f) A copy of the company or partnership accounts (where applicable);
(g) Copies of insurance policies, building society accounts etcetera;
(h) Copies of HP or loan agreements;
(i) Verification of personal loans;
(j) Agreed valuation of matrimonial home;
(k) Agreed valuation of any other piece of property which may be in dispute;
(l) Details of your pension scheme and any death-in-service benefit.

When these lists of documents have been exchanged, inspection of the documents has taken place and both solicitors agree that the matter is ready to be set down for hearing, an application will be made for the matter to be set down for trial with an estimate of the length of time that the trial is going to take.

In due course, the court will allot a date, a time and a registrar to hear the case. Only very complicated financial cases are heard by a judge in the high court (or cases in which the conduct of one or both of the parties is being raised). Before the Matrimonial and Family Proceedings Act (1984), the question of the conduct of the parties did not enter into the financial position unless the conduct was considered by the court to be 'gross and obvious' and that it would be unjust not to take it into consideration when making financial orders. The Matrimonial and Family Proceedings Act (1984) states that the court shall have regard to 'the conduct of each of the parties' if the conduct is such that it would, in the opinion of the court, be unfair to disregard it. In practice, the question of one party's conduct does not affect the financial provision, especially where there are children to be considered, unless there are exceptional or unusual circumstances.

If, after all the relevant information has been exchanged, no agreement can be reached between the parties with the help of their legal advisors, the matter must be dealt with by the court, who will decide on the amount of maintenance and the division of the family's capital assets.

Consent orders

If a final financial agreement has been reached with the help of your advisers, that agreement will be set out in detail in a document known as a minute of order, that is a note of the order which the court will be asked to make. That document, signed by your advisors is lodged at the court at any time after the pronouncement of *decree nisi*, together with a statement which is required by Rule 76A of the Matrimonial Causes Rules.

The court will check that the order is satisfactory and correct given the information it has before it and will make an order in the terms of the minute of order. If you have sworn an affidavit of your means, it is still necessary to complete the statement under Rule 76A. The order granted by the court in this way is known as a consent order.

An application for a consent order for maintenance pending suit or interim periodical payment for the children can be made at any time before *decree absolute*. It is the final financial order which can be made only after the pronouncement of *decree absolute*.

A consent order is more flexible than an order made by the court after a hearing. It indicates by its very nature that there is agreement between the spouses. The consent order can also contain undertakings (promises to the court) such as an undertaking to transfer ownership of various items or the family car. Undertakings are enforceable by the court and breach of an undertaking is taken as seriously as breach of a court order. So do not undertake to do something that you cannot do or have no intention of doing.

Consent orders can be set aside if there has not been full and frank disclosure by one party and that a different settlement or order would have been made if that matter had been disclosed at the time the settlement was agreed and the order made.

Family Law Bar Association (FLBA) Conciliation Board

This is a comparatively new scheme where your respective solicitors may put all the financial information before a barrister, who acts as an informal arbitrator and will make a 'recommendation' as to a reasonable settlement of your case. You are not bound to accept the recommendation unless you both agree to be bound, beforehand or after receiving the recommendation. The scheme can be used only if you both have solicitors and it is sometimes useful to have the opinion of an independent but experienced person which might help achieve a settlement, rather than reaching stalemate and needing the services of a costly court hearing.

The Family Law Bar Association Conciliation Board has set fees. For cases which do not involve substantial capital the fee is £85 and for cases where the capital is more complex, for example where there is a company or partnership and there is quite a lot of financial information to peruse the fee is £150. The legal aid certificate does not cover this scheme.

Details of the scheme can be obtained by your solicitor from the FLBA Conciliation Board, 4 Paper Buildings, Temple, London EC4Y 7EX.

Maintenance

Maintenance is income which you receive from your spouse, either as a voluntary payment or under a court order. In the US, it is known as alimony, and where it relates to children it is known there as child support. In the UK we use the same term 'maintenance' to describe both income for a spouse and income for children. The court and any court order which you may obtain will use the term 'periodical payments order' (ie a payment made to you on a regular, periodical basis) to express this income.

Who receives maintenance?

There is no automatic entitlement to receive maintenace from your spouse, or former spouse. Your claim to maintenance will be determined according to your own source of income (and/or your ability to obtain income for yourself) together with your 'reasonable needs'.

When you first go to see your solicitor, maintenance is one of the financial aspects which he or she will investigate at the interview. You will be asked for a list of your outgoings and for as much information as possible on the financial resources of the family. From this, your solicitor will be able to calculate whether you would be entitled to any maintenance and also whether you require any maintenance. The way in which income may be spread between a spouse and the children in order to obtain the maximum effect of the personal allowances for tax purposes is described later in this chapter. It may be that maintenance is paid to the children of the family and not to the wife, if she is earning, because this is a tax-effective method of giving income to the family unit as a whole. This does not necessarily mean that the wife's claim to maintenance is dismissed. It may be left open even though no maintenance is being paid to her, just in case there are problems in the future and she should, through no fault of her own, lose her own source of income.

If a wife's claim to maintenance is dismissed by the court, with or without her consent, that dismissal is final. She can never go back to the court to ask for maintenance for herself unless her husband failed substantially to disclose his income at the time when the claim to maintenance was dismissed.

It is possible to leave open the claim for maintenance by making a nominal order of 5p per annum where a wife's employment is not secure or her health doubtful. This gives her the ability to apply to the court for maintenance if her circumstances change or make this necessary and desirable.

Paying maintenance to children

There is a statutory duty which falls on both parents to maintain their children. There is no fixed figure or sliding scale for child maintenance; it depends on the joint resources of the parents, and the needs of the child. However, the National Fostercare Association produce figures on an annual basis which give an indication of the cost of bringing up a child in fostercare from birth to 18 years both in London and the provinces. This may help to establish a guide when working out at the cost of maintaining a child. (See Appendix A for the address of The National Fostercare Association). The weekly figures in April 1986 were as follows:

Age of child in years	Recommended allowance in £ per week for provinces	Recommended allowance in £ per week for London
0–4	28.07	31.71
5–7	32.76	37.03
8–10	35.91	40.53
11–12	38.99	44.10
13–15	42.14	47.60
16–18	56.21	63.49

It is always preferable for maintenance payments to a spouse and/or children to be decided by mutual agreement. If no agreement can be reached, then an application must be made to the court for them to determine and decide the amount of maintenance which is to be paid by one spouse to the other spouse and/or the children of the family. If the decree absolute has not been obtained, then the application on the part of the spouse for maintenance is known as an 'application for maintenance pending suit' (ie maintenance pending the finalisation of the divorce proceedings). Until the divorce is final, any order for the children is known as an 'interim periodical payment'.

Refusal to pay maintenance

If your spouse refuses to pay any maintenance whatsoever to you or your children, you must make an application to the court as soon as possible. If there are no divorce proceedings pending, you can make an application on the basis that your spouse has neglected to maintain you or your children. If divorce proceedings have already commenced, you can apply for maintenance pending suit for yourself and interim periodical payments for the children.

Alternatively, you can make an application at any time during the marriage to the magistrates court on the basis that your spouse has failed to maintain you and obtain maintenance payments for you and your children for a three-month initial period, which can be extended to six months.

If your spouse disobeys an order made by the court, and still makes no payment, one possible recourse is to apply to the court for an 'attachment of earnings order'. This application can be made to the court if your spouse is in paid employment with a firm or company. An order is made by the court requiring your spouse's employer to pay, direct to you, the monies due to you and the children by way of maintenance under the previous court order. This payment is made direct from your spouse's monthly salary, after which the balance will be paid to him or her. The order has the effect of ensuring that you receive the income that has been ordered by the court, and the application will often spur an erring spouse into payment, thus making it unnecessary for you to proceed with the application. No one really wishes their personal affairs to be revealed to their employers in this way.

A judgement summons can be issued for arrears of maintenance if it can be shown that the payer has the means to pay maintenance but has refused to do so; in some cases, the payer can be committed to prison. A judgement summons is a useful means of obtaining payment of arrears of maintenance where the payer is self-employed and therefore would be outside the scope of an attachment of earnings order. The threat of a prison sentence and the consequent damage to the self-employed payer's business is usually sufficient to ensure at least an offer of payment of arrears.

Variation of maintenance orders

The court has no power to index link maintenance payments to a spouse and/or children. Some couples agree that the maintenance order should be increased on an annual basis by the percentage increase of the retail price index. If no agreement can be reached between parties on either an increase in the maintenance paid to a spouse and/or children or perhaps, a decrease in maintenance paid to a spouse because of a change of circumstances, then an application must be made for the variation to be determined by the court. An application is made by way of a notice of application supported by an affidavit with up-to-date details of the financial position of the applicant and where possible of the respondent. The procedure through the court is the same as for the first application for financial relief.

There are a number of reasons why a variation might be necessary. In general, applications are made by the spouse with whom the children are living for an increase due merely to the increase of general living expenses and inflation. On the other hand, an application can be made to reduce a spouse's maintenance for various reasons. The payee may have obtained part-time or full-time employment or be receiving income from other sources, the payee may have remarried, the applicant may have remarried perhaps or the payee is cohabiting and the cohabitee is making the financial contribution.

Cohabitation

If, at the time of the determination of the financial application on divorce, one or other spouse is cohabiting with another person and that person has an income and is making a financial contribution to the household, this will be taken into consideration in determining the resources and needs. Similarly if at the time of the determination of the financial application you are cohabiting with another person and substantially supporting that person and/or their children, the level of that support will be taken into consideration – although not to the detriment of the children of the first marriage.

Tax implications of maintenance orders

If maintenance is ordered by the court order during judicial separation or divorce proceedings, the person paying maintenance to the spouse and children will qualify for certain tax advantages. The payment of maintenance to a child under a court order until that child reaches 17 years or ceases full-time education, means that the maintenance is treated as the child's income for tax purposes and not the income of the payer. It is essential when coming to a decision on the amount of income required by various members of the family that all tax allowances are taken into full consideration.

From the day you are born, you are entitled to the single person's allowance (ie income free from tax) which, for the tax year 1986/87, is the sum of £2,335 per annum.

A separated husband can continue to claim the married man's allowance in the year of separation but thereafter must inform the Inland Revenue of the separation and his allowance will be reduced to the single person's allowance. For the year 1986/87 the married man's allowance is £3,655.

A single or separated parent with at least one dependent child who is under 16 years or in full-time education may claim an additional personal allowance which, for the tax year 1986/87, is £1,320. This brings a separated or divorced spouse with a dependent child or children the equivalent of the married man's allowance of £3,655 (£2,335 for the single person's allowance plus £1,320 for the additional personal allowance).

In addition, each child is entitled to the single person's allowance. Therefore, a separated or divorced person with two dependent children can have income of £8,325 per annum before he or she pays a penny in tax. Therefore, it is sensible to divide the total maintenance required by the family between the spouse and children in a tax-effective manner. Subject to small maintenance payments dealt with below, a person paying maintenance deducts tax at the basic rate and sends only the net amount to the payee. The payer is also required to provide tax deduction certificates (Form R185) available from the Inland Revenue office to show that he has done this. So far as the payee is concerned he or she may reclaim from the Inland Revenue any or all of the tax deducted according to his or her own overall income tax liability. This system also applies to child maintenance.

So far as the payer is concerned, this is the mechanism by which he or she obtains basic rate tax relief on the payments. If he or she is a higher rate payer, higher rates of the tax relief are dealt with by the PAYE scheme. Self-employed people at higher rate can reclaim additional relief as part of their annual income tax return.

The person with whom the children are living is also entitled to claim child benefit for each child, which is £7.10 per week per child. This person may also, provided he or she has been separated for a period of 13 weeks and has dependent children, claim the single parent's benefit which stands at £4.60 per week. Therefore, a separated parent with one child can add another £608.40, tax-free, to their income per annum. These benefits are likely to be increased in April 1987, so check the new figures with the DHSS or your local Citizen's Advice Bureau.

Tax relief outside divorce proceedings (deed of separation)

The maintenance for a separated spouse can be dealt with either by way of court order, which can be obtained in the magistrates court, or under a deed of separation. The deed of separation states the date of separation and the agreed amount of maintenance payable by one spouse to another on an annual basis. A maintenance agreement must be capable of lasting for more than 12 months for it to be effective for tax purposes. If a spouse's maintenance is detailed in a deed of separation or under the terms of a court order obtained in the magistrates court, the payer will be entitled to tax relief on these payments at basic rate if he or she is a basic rate tax payer, or at higher rate if he or she is in the higher rate tax bracket. The basic rate of tax for the year 1986/87 is 29%. When paying maintenance to children it is vitally important that it is paid under a court order, as this is the only way that the payer can obtain tax relief on the payments.

A deed of separation detailing maintenance payment to children is insufficient for tax relief purposes. If there are no divorce proceedings, an order with regard to the children's maintenance can be obtained on application in the magistrates court by the custodial parent, or alternatively, on application to the county court under the Guardianship of Minors Acts 1971 and 1973. It is essential that these payments are expressed as being payable to the child and not to an adult on behalf of the child. If the latter is the case the income will be treated as income of the adult payee and the child's single person's allowance cannot be set off against those payments. Payments made to a child which are not under a court order are considered to be the income of the payer and consequently no tax relief can be obtained on them.

Voluntary maintenance payments

A payment made by one spouse to another or to a child, which is not detailed under a court order or a deed of separation, is known as a voluntary maintenance payment. No tax is payable on such a payment by the recipient, nor is the payer entitled to tax relief on it. If, however, the payment is made under a court order or deed of separation, it will attract tax in the payee's hand. Any payment made by a spouse resident abroad to a spouse living in this country is made gross and the payer will not be entitled to tax relief on the payment if he or she is deemed to be non-resident for tax purposes by the Inland Revenue. It is important, therefore, if the payer wishes to take advantage of the tax reliefs, that the payments to a spouse and children are formalised in a deed of separation or court order (spouse) and a court order for the children.

Small maintenance payments

Payments made under a court order, either for the maintenance of a former spouse, or for direct credit to a person under the age of 21 years, are deemed to be small maintenance payments, provided they do not exceed £208 a month or £2,496 a year. These payments are made gross to the former spouse or child that is without the payer having deducted tax at basic rate. Any payment made to a former spouse or child over and above that amount is paid under deduction of basic rate tax.

So it is important, when reaching a decision as to how much income is required by a former spouse and dependent children and how that income is to be paid, that you consider the requirement of the deduction of tax at basic rate from payments made to a spouse or child over and above £2,496 per annum. Small maintenance payments, because they are paid gross to the payee, help the cashflow in that the payee does not have to wait to receive any tax which he or she may be able to reclaim from the Inland Revenue.

Example 1

A payment of £5,000 per annum maintenance under a deed of separation or court order, to a spouse living with a dependent child will attract tax of £390.05 per annum provided that spouse does not have any other income from any other source.

The calculation is as follows:

Income	£5,000
(Deduct single person's allowance)	£2,335
Sub-total	£2,665
(Deduct additional personal allowance)	£1,320
Total taxable income	£1,345

Tax payable on £1,345 at 29% is £390.05 a year

Fixing a sum for maintenance

In determining the amount of income required to be paid to a former spouse and children of the family, the courts tend toward a practical approach based on the needs of each parent, the needs of the children, and the resources (including the tax relief) of each parent available to provide for the needs. The use of what is known as the 'one third guideline' is decreasing, although where there are substantial income resources, it is a useful starting point. The one third guideline offers a basis for determining the amount of maintenance required. It is a guideline only and not a rule. Calculate one third of the joint income of the parties and use this figure as a guideline for maintenance payable.

Example 2

Take the husband's gross monthly pay and deduct National Insurance contributions, pension contribution if this is compulsory and the cost of his travel to work. This will leave £X per month.

Take the wife's gross monthly pay together with child benefit and deduct National Insurance contributions, pension contributions if compulsory, cost of travel to work and the cost of childcare. This will leave £Y per month.

Combine £X and £Y and divide by 3 = £⅓ of joint incomes.

It is now generally considered to be more helpful to look at the needs of the family and the resources available to supply those needs. A basic calculation must be performed to establish the income of the household as it stands and the estimated outgoing of the new households. In the example below the household expenditure is calculated on the requirements of a family with a mother and two children:

Expenses	Cost per calendar month in £
Mortgage	200
Rates	40
Water Rates	5
Gas	40
Electricity	20
Telephone	20
Food and Household necessities	250
House Insurance	5
Life Insurance Policy	10
Mortgage Protection Policy	5
Car Tax	8
Car Insurance	12
Petrol	40
General repairs to house and household equipment	30
Holidays	60
Clothes	65
Entertainment	65
Fares	40
Total	847

The calculation reveals that this family requires a net income of £10,164 per annum. Making use of the children's single person's tax free allowance, maintenance can be paid to the children at a rate of £2,335 per annum, giving a total payment to both children of £4,670 per annum. A further £5,494 must be found either from the wife's resources or from the husband's or from a combination of the two.

We must take into consideration child benefit for the two children at £728 a year for both and the single parent's allowance for the separated or divorced mother living with two dependent children. This will give another £236.60 a year leaving a balance of £4,530 to find. Let us say that the husband will pay maintenance to the spouse of £3,655 a year (which is the single person's allowance combined with an additional person's allowance) leaving her with a shortfall of £875. This can be made up by the spouse taking a lodger into the spare room for which she will charge £25 per week, giving her an extra £1,300 a year. Because her personal tax relief has been eaten up in the maintenance paid to her by her husband, it will be necessary for her to pay tax on this sum at the rate of £377 a year.

Every maintenance case is slightly different, and it will be judged by the court on its own merits. Here are three examples of how specific situations are generally treated.

Example 3

Ben and Amelia have been married for two years and have decided to separate. They are both working. Amelia earns £8,000 a year as a secretary and Ben earns £9,500 a year as a bank clerk. Amelia is 24 years old and Ben is 26. The marriage is short, there are no children, and both Amelia and Ben earn enough money to support themselves on separation without requiring maintenance from the other.

In this situation, Amelia would be advised that she has no grounds to claim maintenance from Ben and that she should consent to her claim for maintenance being dismissed on the basis that Ben's potential claim for maintenance would also be dismissed. If Amelia refused to accept this advice and insisted on going ahead with her claim for maintenance against Ben, it is highly probable that her claim would be dismissed in any event by the registrar who heard the matter. Both Ben and Amelia are perfectly able to support themselves on their salaries and there is no reason why either should preserve their claim against the other in the future. If Amelia pursued her claim for maintenance, she may well be ordered to pay Ben's legal costs as well as her own.

Example 4

Cecil is chief executive of a bank and earns £40,000. He is 63 years old. Ethel, his wife, is 61 and has not worked for 27 years. Their children are now grown up and married. Cecil and Ethel decide to separate and divorce proceedings commence.

Ethel's maintenance would be based on consideration of both her 'reasonable needs' and the standard of living to which she has become accustomed. Ethel could probably expect to receive a maintenance order in the region of £8,000 to £12,000 per annum. There would be no question of dismissal of her claim to maintenance and Cecil would be expected to maintain her until her death or remarriage. It may be, however, that Cecil had accumulated sufficient capital during the marriage to enable him to make a lump sum payment to Ethel sufficient for her to invest, and obtain income from, for the rest of her life. But it is more likely that Ethel's claim to maintenance would remain live during her lifetime, although her income may decrease somewhat when Cecil finally retired.

Example 5 (maintenance to children from another marriage)

When Amy met Bob, she was divorced from her first husband and had two children by him, Harry and Alice. Amy's first husband was last heard of about three years ago, when he emigrated to Australia and she has been unable to contact him since or to enforce the maintenance order for Harry and Alice. Bob, when he married Amy, was perfectly happy to take on Harry and Alice and to support them as members of the family. Bob and Amy then had a further child, George.

Bob, in these circumstances, will have been deemed to have treated Harry and Alice as children of the family. He has accepted them as part of the family and has supported them as such. In this case, it is quite possible that an order for maintenance could be made against Bob in respect of Harry, Alice and George.

Do not assume that because the children are not your natural children, you will not have to pay maintenance to them in the event of a divorce.

Other contributing factors

The court, in exercising its powers to make financial orders on a decree of divorce will look not only at the parties' needs (and resources to supply those needs) but also, where relevant, the following factors.

(a) The income, earning capacity, property and other financial resources which each party has or is likely to have in the foreseeable future, including any increase in a party's earning capacity which it would be reasonable for the court to expect that party to acquire;

This relates to the ability, for example, of a wife who up until the separation or divorce has remained at home looking after the children and who may now be able to find some remunerative employment.

(b) The financial needs, obligations and responsibilities which each of the parties has or is likely to have in the foreseeable future;

This relates to any future liability a party may have to support a second wife or child of that union and any future resource which a party is likely to acquire.

(c) The standard of living enjoyed by the family before the breakdown of marriage;

Clearly, in many cases it is very difficult for two households to live at the same standard as the original family unit but the needs and expectations of that family must be considered. If, for example, it was always envisaged that the children should be educated in the private sector, consideration should be given to this factor, when calculating the division of the family finances.

(d) The age of the parties and the length of the marriage;
(e) Any physical or mental disability of either party to the marriage;
(f) The contribution which each party has made or is likely to make in the future to the welfare of the family;

This does not relate only to financial contributions but also to the contribution which a wife makes in remaining in the home, cooking, cleaning and bringing up the children.

(g) The conduct of each of the parties, if that conduct is such that it would in the opinion of the court be inequitable to disregard it;

There has been much argument and discussion in legal circles as to whether this particular phrase which deals with the conduct of the parties would open the flood-gate and bring numerous applications in which a party based a financial claim substantially on the 'bad conduct' of the other party. There is no specific definition of 'conduct' but it would have to be serious before the court would take it into consideration as a penalising factor on one party.

(h) Where there are proceedings for divorce or nullity, the value to each of the parties of any benefit (for example pension) which, through divorce or annulment, that party would lose the chance of acquiring.

The question of loss of pension rights or rights to the value on insurance policies is extremely important, particularly in divorces between older people, and you should discuss these matters with your solicitor.

Financial provision in the magistrates court

An application for maintenance and/or a lump sum can be made in the magistrates court provided that:
1 Both parties reside in England and Wales; or
2 The respondent to the application resides in Scotland or Northern Ireland and the applicant in England and Wales and the parties last ordinarily resided in England and Wales together as man and wife; or
3 The applicant resides in Scotland or Northern Ireland and the respondent resides in England and Wales.

The application can be made if either party to a marriage has:
1 Failed to provide reasonable maintenance for the applicant or any children of the family;
2 Behaved in such a way that the applicant cannot reasonably be expected to live with him or her;
3 The respondent has deserted the applicant.

The court can order maintenance to the applicant and children and a lump sum of a maximum £500 to the applicant and to each child.

Under section 7 of the Domestic Proceedings and Magistrates Court Act, if the parties to a marriage have been apart for three months and one party has paid maintenance to the applicant or a child of the family, the applicant may apply for an order for maintenance.

It is this section which can be used to obtain an order for children's maintenance in order to take advantage of tax relief where the parties have separated and a deed of separation has been used to detail the agreement reached. A spouse's maintenance in a deed of separation will attract tax relief.

Debts and liabilities

The court will consider the whole financial picture before making financial orders on divorce. This includes consideration of the family debts and liabilities and also of the debts and liabilities of the individual. Most families have an overdraft at the bank, a hire purchase agreement and credit card liabilities. However, while repayment of these debts must be taken into consideration, on the whole, the courts will consider only 'necessary debts'. So there is little point in embarking on a wild spending spree and building up vast debts in order to defeat your spouse's claim, or more importantly your children's claim, to maintenance and capital.

Most couples have a joint bank account and/or savings accounts. If you are separated or even divorced, you are still jointly liable for any indebtedness on these accounts. For this reason, it is wise, on separation, to close all joint accounts and to open separate accounts in your own name. If you cannot agree on the division of the money in any savings accounts, it is wise to 'freeze' those accounts until agreement can be reached. This is easily done by writing to the appropriate bank or building society informing them of the separation or intended separation and requesting that there be no withdrawals from the account without the permission of both account holders. It is always wise to inform your bank and building societies of the separation and ask that no money should be drawn without both signatures, just in case your spouse decides to clear the savings account and to embark on a spending spree.

Household debts

It is quite likely, when experiencing separation and divorce, for a household to build up arrears on rates, electricity, gas and telephone accounts and on insurance policy premiums. When money is tight – perhaps your spouse is not paying any maintenance and you are still waiting for the matter to be decided by the court – the obvious 'economy' may be to ignore the household bills. Alternatives may be that your spouse has agreed to pay the household bills and you are in blissful ignorance that he or she has not done so until you receive notice that you are about to be cut off or the bailiff appears at your door. Great care should be taken to avoid this.

Rates

The spouse responsible for paying the rates in the past will continue to be responsible until *decree absolute* even if he or she is not actually living in the property. The spouse responsible for payment can be sued for non-payment of rates by the local authority who have the right to send in the bailiff to take away goods to the value of the debt. In these circumstances, it is wise to contact the local authority as soon as you know of the debt to see if it is possible to arrange to pay the arrears by instalments. Alternatively, if there is an order or even agreement that your spouse should pay the rates, you should contact your solicitor either about enforcement proceedings in respect of that order, or about obtaining an order from the court confirming the agreement.

The divisional court has held that if a husband pays maintenance to a wife to include rates and if she does not use that money for that purpose she can be made liable for non-payment of rates.

Electricity, gas and telephone accounts

It is always wise to contact your local office as soon as you are aware that there are arrears on electricity, gas or telephone accounts. Failure to settle these accounts will eventually lead to you being cut off. Explain the situation to the accounts manager in the appropriate office and ask not be cut off. Again, you may be able to pay the arrears by instalments or alternatively, the DHSS may be in a position to help you with the bills.

There is a useful leaflet **How To Get Help if you Can't Pay your Bill** available from the Electricity and Gas Boards.

Insurance policy premiums

There is a tendency when you are short of money, to stop paying the premium on, for example, your house contents insurance or mortgage protection policy. It is a false economy and, in most cases, it is advisable to resist the temptation. If you stop paying the premiums it is tantamount to cancelling the policy and if you then have a burglary you will not be able to claim on your policy. The maintenance which you receive from your spouse combined with your own income resources should be sufficient to cover these payments. If you are not receiving sufficient income, consult your solicitor immediately.

Mortgage arrears

Where there are substantial arrears of mortgage repayments, a bank or building society may institute proceedings for possession in which case the house will be placed on the market for sale and the outstanding mortgage, on sale, repaid to the lender. A building society or other lender entitled to sell by virtue of an order of possession is required to obtain only a reasonable market price for the property which is not necessarily the best price. It is therefore most important that you avoid possession proceedings if at all possible.

Contact the building society as soon as you know of the arrears and explain the position to them. It may be that the house is going to be sold in any event as a result of the separation and in such circumstances a building society will often agree to let you sell the property thus ensuring the best price. If a wife has registered a charge on the home to protect her right of occupation under the Matrimonial Homes Act, she will be notified of possession proceedings by the building society which is under a statutory duty to give such notice. However, if no charge has been registered and the property and mortgage is in the sole name of the husband, the wife will not necessarily know of the proceedings.

Rented property

A wife has the right, under the Matrimonial Homes Act, to live in rented property which is in her husband's sole name up to *decree absolute*. If the landlord commences possession proceedings against a husband for arrears of rent the wife must take legal advice and apply to be joined as a defendant in the proceedings. The wife would also be wise to contact her local housing department and seek advice in case of eviction. If there are dependent children, then the wife's case would be given priority with regard to rehousing.

The alimony drone – myth or reality?

There was a great deal of discussion shortly before the Matrimonial and Family Proceedings Act (1984) became law as to whether it was the case that on separation and divorce women 'milked' their husbands of money. In my experience, 'the alimony drone' is a rare breed and most divorced women with dependent children find it hard to manage on their former husband's maintenance, even when it is supplemented by their own efforts to obtain employment and alternative sources of income.

It is reasonable to expect a woman to contribute her own income resources towards the needs of the family but consideration must be given to each case on its merits. Often a woman will have given up her job in order to look after the children (at her husband's request or by mutual decision) and as such she will have given up valuable career prospects and have fallen behind as far as potential income from employment is concerned. Alternatively, whatever her past experience, a woman who has been out of the work market for some time will find it more difficult to obtain employment than someone who has remained in it. Furthermore, consideration must be given to the ages and the demands of the children. If the mother goes out to work, childcare facilities may have to be organised and paid for. Many couples find that the expense of childcare, the time-consuming demands of children (even if they are looked after by someone else all day) and the difficulties of finding a well-paid job after several years out of the market make it economically unviable for the mother to consider working until the children are at least in full-time education. On the whole, the courts are giving full consideration to these matters and will look at the circumstances of each case on its merits.

If you remarry, the income and capital of your second spouse can be taken into account when calculating a maintenance and capital order for the first spouse and children. A second spouse is not liable to subsidise a first spouse. However if, for example, the original husband and wife had limited resources and one or other remarries someone much richer, that will inevitably affect the extent to which that party can make any claim for capital resources based on need.

So far as income is concerned the relevance of a second spouse is as to whether or not they can pay their way.

Example 1 – Capital
Henry and Wendy have a house in joint names valued at £60,000 with a mortgage of £20,000. There are two children. Henry has left Wendy and married Ann who has a house of her own. Henry therefore has accommodation and no immediate need for capital to rehouse himself. In this case it would be possible for the matrimonial home to be transferred to Wendy in full and final settlement of her capital claim against Henry. Ann's house will in effect have been taken into consideration as accommodation for Henry.

Example 2 – Income
Henry has an income of £20,000 a year and Ann has an income of £15,000 a year. Ann's income is used to pay the mortgage on the house and the food. This releases Henry of some of the burden of financing

two households and leaves more of his income to support Wendy and the children.

The clean break

The concept of the 'clean break' is one favoured not only by husbands but also, to an increasing extent, by wives. The clean break refers to a financial settlement where both parties' claims are satisfied and dismissed and no further payments made by one to the other.

The Matrimonial and Family Proceedings Act (1984) increases the possibility of a clean break settlement by giving the court the power to direct a wife's claim against her husband for continuing maintenance to be dismissed, without first requiring the wife's consent. The courts are using this new power carefully and it is most unlikely that a wife with young and still dependent children, who has been out of employment for some years, would have her claim to maintenance dismissed. Similarly, a woman in her 50s who has always been a wife and mother and has never been employed will rarely have her claim for maintenance dismissed.

The clean break principle may be used where there is sufficient capital available to compensate the wife for any loss of maintenance or pension rights. For example, a wife may be awarded a large lump sum sufficient to invest and obtain an income from, to cover her needs both present and future. In these circumstances, the clean break is viable only if one can be sure that the future and long-term needs of the wife can be catered for.

In some cases, a spouse's interest in the matrimonial home may be transferred into the other spouse's sole name in full and final settlement of all claims – this again, would be a clean break settlement.

Lump sum

A lump sum is a payment of cash from one spouse to the other. Once the sum has been paid, the recipient cannot claim any further lump sums. If the matrimonial home is not sold but one spouse intends to 'buy out' the other, this payment is often expressed as a lump sum payment.

Any one-off payment of cash is a lump sum payment. For example, a payment to a wife of £10,000 which is to be invested by her in an annuity to produce an income or capital sum for her old age would be expressed as a lump sum. Or, a cash payment made to a wife instead of continuing maintenance may be expressed as a lump sum.

A lump sum order may be made in favour of children but if this occurs it will normally be necessary for trustees to be appointed to manage the money and its investment until the children are of age.

Any income produced by a lump sum, whether for a spouse or

children, will be taken into consideration when calculating maintenance.

If you are in receipt of a legal aid certificate, a lump sum, if it exceeds £25,000, can attract the statutory charge. The Law Society will exercise the statutory charge immediately and will require your solicitor to retain the lump sum pending the final determination of the bill of legal costs.

The matrimonial home
'Matrimonial home' is a term used to describe a home which is owned or rented by either or both spouses and lived in during the course of the marriage by the family.

Who lives in the matrimonial home prior to an agreement being reached or an order made?
There are no set rules to follow regarding who remains in the matrimonial home and who goes, pending an agreement as to what is to be done with it. It depends very much on individual circumstances, although it is fair to say that if there are children involved, the court gives first consideration to the welfare of the children. So it is more than likely that they will stay in the home with the parent who generally looks after them.

It is quite possible for both spouses to continue living in the same property for some period pending an agreement as to what is to happen to the matrimonial home or an order of the court relating to the home. It is possible, although fairly unusual, for the parties to be divorced whilst still living under the same roof, albeit separately.

Dealing with the privately-owned matrimonial home on separation or divorce
The matrimonial home tends to be the main family asset in most cases and there are three methods of dealing with it on a separation and divorce.

(a) The home can be sold and the proceeds of sale divided by agreement or by order of the court;
(b) The ownership of the home can be transferred from one spouse to another outright;
(c) The sale of the home can be postponed until a later date when the proceeds will be divided in the proportions agreed.

There are no set rules or guidelines as to whether the house is to be sold, ownership transferred, or sale postponed. Nor are there any set guidelines as to the proportion in which the proceeds of sale should be divided. The disposal or division of the matrimonial home will depend on the circumstances of the family, the length of the marriage, the age of the parties, the age and number of children and any other relevant factors. On separation or divorce the primary issue is working out a way of housing the family in two households as opposed to one.

Where the property is held in joint names and in the absence of a written statement declaring that the owners hold the beneficial interest in the property in unequal proportions each party is strictly entitled to 50% of the equity, that is the balance of the value of the property after deducting the amount of the outstanding mortgage and possibly any other charge registered on the property. However, in reality, and particularly where there are children involved, the court must decide whether it would be fair and just for the equity to be divided equally, given that both parties must be rehoused and one party will certainly have to rehouse the children as well.

Where the house is in a spouse's sole name, let us say the husband's, the wife under the matrimonial law will generally have a claim to part of the equity but this will depend again on all the circumstances: length of the marriage, number of children, age of parties, wife's contribution (whether in money terms or otherwise). The needs of the family and the resources available to provide these needs will always be the deciding factor.

Sale of the home

Where there are no children and both parties are in remunerative employment, it is likely that the matrimonial home would be sold and the net proceeds of the sale divided either by agreement or in proportions ordered by the court. The sale of the home is most common where the marriage is relatively short and both parties can obtain independent mortgages which, together with their share of the net proceeds, will purchase alternative accommodation.

If one spouse wishes to remain in the matrimonial home it may be possible for that spouse to 'buy out' the other's interest on an agreed valuation of that interest, and remain there then by increasing the mortgage or taking out a second loan.

Where there are children to accommodate and there is sufficient equity in the matrimonial home to make it economically viable to sell it, pay off the mortgage, pay for legal and estate agent fees, and rehouse the wife and children (paying for the expenses of purchase with the net proceeds of sale) then the court may order an immediate sale. It may be economic to do this because it releases the husband of the burden of mortgage repayments on the matrimonial home and may even release to him a small lump sum to use as a deposit on alternative accommodation for himself.

Generally, the court will order a sale of the matrimonial home only if it is satisfied that there will be sufficient monies, after repayment of the outstanding mortgage and expenses of sale, to purchase suitable alternative accommodation at least for the spouse with whom the children are living, and if possible for both spouses.

Transfer of ownership from one spouse to the other

Transferring the ownership of the matrimonial home from joint names to a sole name or from the sole name of one spouse to the sole name of the other would generally occur in a situation where the clean break is envisaged.

For example: a wife agrees to take the whole of the equity of the matrimonial home in full and final settlement of all her claims to capital against the husband, where the matrimonial home is not the only capital asset of the family. The husband would in this case transfer to the wife his interest in the property whether it is in his sole name or in joint names.

An alternative example exists where the wife may agree to take the husband's interest in the matrimonial home, which would then be transferred into her sole name in full and final settlement of all her claims against him as to capital and maintenance. Generally, this would happen only if the wife were in a position to maintain and therefore remain in the property or if she would receive sufficient monies from the sale to rehouse herself and any children, and if the husband is able to provide himself with alternative accommodation.

Postponed sale

This is the most usual order in respect of the matrimonial home where there are young dependent children and where there is insufficient equity in the property to render viable a sale and the purchase of alternative accommodation for one or both parties.

In these circumstances the court will usually make an order that the wife remain in the matrimonial home until one of the following events occurs:

(a) The wife remarries;
(b) The wife cohabits (usually for a period of six months or more);
(c) The youngest child reaches the age of 16 or 18 years;
(d) Earlier sale;
(e) A specific date (any period which the court may specify).

Sometimes a sale is indefinitely postponed. In certain circumstances the husband, the court says, should retain some interest in the property but will not put any definite limit on the period in which the wife can remain there. If this happens, it is made a term of the order that the husband may make an application to the court for sale of the property if his circumstances change.

When the first of these events occurs, the house is sold and the net proceeds of sale divided between the spouses in the proportions specified by the court. The court will decide the proportions on the basis of the circumstances and projected circumstances of both parties but always bearing in mind that when the home is eventually sold the wife will have to rehouse herself. It is for this reason that even in the case of a postponed sale, the wife may be awarded two-thirds or even three-quarters of the equity if this is what she will need to rehouse herself at that time.

The postponed sale has the effect of providing suitable accommodation for the children (and wife) but also of tying up the capital of the husband. The husband cannot use his proportion of the equity as collateral or security for a loan, for example.

If the matrimonial home is in the husband's sole name it is likely that the court would order it to be transferred in one of two ways:

(a) Into joint names (this is a protection for the wife because the house could not be sold without both signatures);
(b) Into the wife's sole name (the court order being sufficient to preserve the husband's entitlement to his share of the equity).

The latter is more usual where there is a mortgage on the property, in which case the mortgage, too, is transferred into the wife's sole name (with the consent of the lender or building society). The reason for this is to enable the husband to obtain a mortgage for himself, in order to purchase alternative accommodation. Nearly all building societies and banks will refuse a loan or mortgage for the purchase of property if the prospective borrower already has a prior mortgage commitment. When the house is eventually sold and the husband receives his share there may well be a liability to capital gains tax if the house is still in joint names.

Mortgages and tax relief

An individual is entitled to tax relief at 29% on the interest payable on a loan of up to £30,000 to purchase or improve his or her home. The tax relief is given at source and the repayment which you make each month will be the net payment. This is known as the MIRAS Scheme (Mortgage Interest Relief At Source).

If, however, your loan exceeds £30,000 the gross amount is payable each month and tax relief will be given on the first £30,000 only, by way of your tax code.

If you transfer the matrimonial home into your spouse's sole name together with the mortgage, but you are still paying the mortgage repayments, make sure that the amount of the mortgage repayments are made to your spouse by way of maintenance to him or her. In this way, your spouse will be entitled to tax relief on the mortgage repayments and you will be entitled to tax relief on the payment of maintenance made to your spouse. You will also be in the position of being able to take out your own mortgage if you wish and to receive tax relief on the loan up to £30,000.

Stamp duty

Transfers of property valued at more than £30,000 will be subject to one per cent stamp duty. All transfers of property taking place after 26 March 1985 which are part of a court order in divorce proceedings or judicial separation proceedings are subject to a nominal 50 pence stamp duty.

The matrimonial home – rights of occupation and protection from sale

If you and your spouse have joint ownership of your home, you normally have a right to half the equity of the property and the right to occupy the property. If you do not own any interest in the property you still have a right to continue living there, or if you are not actually living there, you have the right, with the agreement of the court, to return and live in the home.

If the home is in your spouse's name you can stop the property being sold without your knowledge by registering on the title deeds your right to occupation, which warns a prospective purchaser that there is a potential dispute relating to the property and that he or she may not be purchasing a clear title. You should register your rights as soon as possible and you are advised to consult a solicitor.

The type of notice required for registering your rights will depend on whether your property is registered or unregistered. If the property is registered you should register a notice on Form 99 which is available from the government bookshops. The form should be lodged at the Land Registry (see Appendix A). The Land Registry publish a booklet which explains the process. You will need to know the title number of the property and the full name of the registered proprietor, the title number can be obtained by doing a map-index search at the Land Registry or, if there is a mortgage on the property, the mortgagee (building society or bank) will hold the title deeds and will be able to tell you the title number.

If the property is unregistered then a Class F land charge should be registered against the title at the Land Charges Department (see Appendix A). You will be required to give the full name of the person who owns the property and a description of the property.

The effect of the registration of a notice or Class F land charge usually lapses once there is *decree absolute* and this may be a reason to delay an application for *decree absolute*. However if a transfer of property application in respect of the specific property has already been made, a charge can be registered on the strength of this, which has the same effect.

If there are problems in your marriage which you consider may lead to separation and divorce and your name is not on the title deeds of the property you should consider registering a notice or Class F land charge in order to protect your rights of occupation against third parties.

It is unlikely that a building society or bank or other lender would give your spouse a mortgage or loan secured on the matrimonial home if a notice or Class F land charge has been registered on the title deeds, thus protecting the equity in the property and your potential share of that equity.

Household contents

On separation and/or divorce it will be necessary to divide the contents of the house between you. Where at all possible this should be done by agreement. The division of contents can often lead to problems and acrimony and all efforts should be made to reach a reasonable and amicable arrangement.

One way of doing this is by each of you making a list of the items in the matrimonial home which you want and seeing which of these items can be agreed on. In doing this, you should consider each other's needs; for example, certain items will be necessary for the person with whom the children will be living (freezer, washing machine, etc). This method will generally leave you with a list of unagreed items which can be dealt with at a later date either by agreement or ultimately by the court.

Try to organise as much as you can by yourselves without involving solicitors. Using legal advice to obtain a decision as to who should have the antique coal scuttle is an expensive business. As a guideline, the following provisions generally apply when the court deals with the division of contents:

(a) Pieces owned by each party before the marriage remain the property of that person.
(b) Any piece bought by one party with his or her own money during the marriage remains the property of that person.
(c) Wedding presents and other gifts remain with the person from whose friends or relations they came.
(d) Items bought with joint money or for the family – for example a

washing machine – are jointly owned and must be divided by agreement or by order of the court.

If the ownership of property is in dispute an application can be made under section 17 of the Married Women's Property Act 1882 by either spouse at any time up to three years after *decree absolute*. The court, under this act can give a declaration only as to who is the owner of the property and order that property to be handed to the owner or sold if the court finds that the property is jointly owned.

The court within divorce proceedings can make orders with regard to contents under the property adjustment provision and it is better to deal with contents, if possible, in this way.

Other capital assets

Apart from the matrimonial home there may be other capital assets in the family which must be divided and dealt with on divorce. For example, a holiday home (abroad or in this country), cars, a boat, a caravan, stocks, shares, insurance policies, jewellery, livestock.

There are no hard and fast rules as to how these assets should be assigned but it will depend upon factors like: the ownership of the assets, who paid for them, were they a gift from one spouse to another? The following rules generally apply:

(a) Savings in joint names should be divided equally unless they are to be used to repay debts or for the purchase of alternative accommodation.
(b) Savings in a sole name would remain with that person unless, for example, a lump sum is required by a wife for investment in an annuity to compensate for loss of pension rights.
(c) The burden and benefit of insurance policies should be divided fairly given the needs and resources of each party.

It used to be the case that, after dealing with the matrimonial home and joint assets, a wife may be awarded up to one-third of the husband's capital. However, these days the court tends towards a more egalitarian approach and will make orders on the basis of the reasonable needs of the wife and the ability of the husband to meet those reasonable needs.

The disposal of assets in order to defeat a spouse's claim

Sometimes, one party considers that the other party may be disposing of assets prior to the commencement of or during divorce proceedings in order substantially to reduce the assets and consequently his or her spouse's entitlement to these assets.

If some evidence for this suspicion can be supplied, then an application can be made to the court, supported by an affidavit, for an order restraining the suspected party from further disposing of assets. It is also possible to freeze certain assets and accounts although this must not be done to the extent that it might seriously affect the spouse's business.

The burden of proof is on the suspected party to satisfy the court that the disposal of assets was made, for example, in the ordinary course of business and not with a view to defeating the other party's claim.

Capital gains tax

Capital gains tax may be payable on various assets which you may need to sell on divorce in order to provide cash for a lump sum payment, for example. Assets which may attract capital gains tax include: stocks, shares, a second home, an interest in a business.

In the tax year 1986/87 an individual may realise a gain of up to £6,300 without incurring a liability to capital gains tax. A married couple share this exemption between them. A husband is assessed on his personal gains during the year of separation and on his own and his wife's gains up to the date of separation. Capital gains tax is payable on various assets which you may need to sell on divorce in order to provide cash for a lump sum payment, for example. Assets which may attract capital gains tax include: stocks, shares, a second home, an interest in a business.

In the tax year 1986/87 an individual may realise a gain of up to £6,300 without incurring a liability to capital gains tax. A married couple share this exemption between them. A husband is assessed on his personal gains during the year of separation and on his own and his wife's gains up to the date of separation. Capital gains tax is payable at the rate of 30%. In assessing gains, inflation is taken into account using the increase in the retail prices index.

The main problems with regard to liability for capital gains tax within the context of a divorce will arise in the following situations.

(a) On the sale of the matrimonial home, if postponed. If there is to be a postponed sale of the matrimonial home, and the home has been transferred into the wife's sole name, there may be a liability to capital gains tax on the part of the husband when he eventually realises his share, if either the property is not his principal private residence (which would exempt him from capital gains tax) or the husband has not lived in the house for minimum of two years;
(b) On the sale of a second or holiday home.

Generally this cannot be said to be your principal private residence and as such any gains made on sale in excess of £6,300 will be liable to capital gains tax.

(c) On the sale of stocks and/or shares to pay out a lump sum.

The sale of any stocks and shares to pay a lump sum to a wife will attract a liability to capital gains tax on any gain in excess of £6,300.

(d) On the sale of all or part of a business.

The sale of all or part of a business to raise cash on divorce may give rise to a liability to capital gains tax.

It would be wise for you to take specialist advice about capital gains tax from your solicitor or an accountant. The following example shows how liability to capital gains tax may arise on divorce.

Example 7
Peter and Jane own the matrimonial home in joint names, valued at £100,000 with outstanding mortgage at the time of the financial settlement of divorce at £30,000. So there is an equity of £70,000, which is insufficient to rehouse Jane and their two children, Frank and Jim. It is agreed that Jane and the children will remain in the matrimonial home until the youngest, Jim, reaches 17 years of age. At this point, the house will be sold and Peter will get one third of the net proceeds of the sale, which on present figures would be £23,333.

If at the time of the sale of the matrimonial home, Peter has purchased his own accommodation, the Inland Revenue would be entitled to charge capital gains tax on his share or the increase in value of the house. However, there is a limited relief in respect of inflation and also an annual personal exemption.

Capital transfer tax/inheritance tax

Since the 1986 budget and the commencement of the tax year 1986/87 on 6 April, capital transfer tax has been substantially changed. Capital transfer tax has been replaced by an inheritance tax which took effect from March 17, 1986. This tax applies to transfers on or within seven years before death, although there is a reduction in the tax payable on transfers between seven and three years before death. The annual exemption of £3,000 per annum for lifetime transfer remains unchanged.

Financial relief – the foreign element

Before the Matrimonial and Family Proceedings Act (1984), parties who had obtained a decree of divorce outside England and Wales were not able to apply to the court in England and Wales either for financial relief or for their financial position to be decided on, or following, a decree of divorce. However, the Matrimonial and Family Proceedings Act (1984) Part III, which is now in force, allows applications to be made to the courts in England and Wales following an overseas divorce, where a marriage has been dissolved or annulled or the parties legally separated in judicial or other proceedings in an overseas country and the divorce, annulment, or legal separation is recognised as valid in England and Wales. (If after a marriage or annulment abroad one of the parties remarries, that party is not entitled to make an application for financial relief.)

It is necessary to obtain the leave of the court before making an application for financial relief in these circumstances and the court will hear the preliminary issues and grant leave to make the application only if it is satisfied that there are substantial grounds for making such an application. The court can give leave for the application even if a financial order has already been made by another court outside England and Wales.

If the court considers that there is an immediate need for financial assistance for the applicant or any child of the family, an interim order for maintenance can be made. The court is able to make financial orders provided that one of the following criteria is satisfied:

(a) Either of the parties to the marriage was domiciled in England and Wales on the date of the application for leave or on the date that the divorce, annulment or legal separation took effect in the overseas country;
(b) Either of the parties to the marriage was habitually resident in England and Wales for a period of one year immediately before the application or the date on which the divorce, annulment or legal separation took effect in the overseas country;
(c) Either or both of the parties to the marriage had, at the date of the application for leave, a beneficial interest in possession of a dwelling house situated in England and Wales which was at some time during the marriage a matrimonial home of the parties.

Before a court will make a financial order in these circumstances, it will take into consideration a number of factors:

(a) The connection of the parties to England and Wales;

(b) The country in which the divorce, annulment or legal separation took place;
(c) Any financial award or benefit already received or likely to be received by the applicant or any child as a consequence of a divorce, annulment, legal separation or agreement in another country;
(d) The extent to which any order made by the court will be enforceable on a practical basis;
(e) The length of time which has elapsed since the date of the divorce, annulment or legal separation;
(f) Any right which the applicant has and may not have exercised to apply for financial relief in any country outside England and Wales.

Under Part III of the Matrimonial and Family Proceedings Act (1984), the court may make any or all of the following orders:

(a) Periodical payments order (maintenance);
(b) Secured periodical payments order;
(c) Lump sum order;
(d) Property adjustment order.

Where the court grants the applicant in these circumstances leave to make an application to the court for financial relief and at the same time is satisfied that a party is disposing of assets with a view to defeating the other party's financial claim, the court has the same power to make orders restraining that party from disposing of assets and protecting the potential financial claim.

The act also allows a financial claim to be made in the Scottish courts after an overseas divorce (a decree of divorce obtained in England and Wales would be regarded by the Scottish courts as an 'overseas divorce').

Chapter 7

Other financial provisions

Loss of pension rights on divorce

A word of warning to wives: you will lose your right, on *decree absolute*, to any part of your husband's pension on retirement, to a widow's pension and to part of your state pension. (Although you may be able to draw a reduced state pension at the age of 60, based on the contributions which your husband made during the years that you were married.) A divorced woman under the age of 60 can add her former husband's contributions to her own if that would give her a larger state pension or enable her to qualify for a state pension. If she marries again before age 60 she can no longer use her former husband's contributions. Alternatively, if you have been employed in the past and contributed yourself to a pension fund, then this contribution will remain good after your divorce.

The question of loss of pension rights is especially important for women in their 50s and 60s. Make sure that your solicitor gives full consideration to your position with regard to this point. The loss of pension rights for a woman in her early or late 30s or even early 40s is not something that can be realistically quantified in the case of most women. However, if, for example, you suffer from an illness which may gradually incapacitate you in later life, this is an important factor to be taken into consideration in any financial settlement. The DHSS produce two very good pamphlets about pensions. NI.1 is the pamphlet for married women and NI.51 is the one for widows. You will find these at your local social security office or from the DHSS Leaflets Unit (see Appendix A).

You may consider a lump sum, if this is appropriate, as compensation for the loss of pension rights. Some or all of this could then be invested in, for example, a capital accumulation scheme which would provide an income for the investor in old age. Alternatively, you may wish to consider taking out an insurance policy on your ex-husband's life. If you do this, remember to build the cost of the premium into any maintenance provision he may make. It is important to discuss the problem of loss of pension rights with your solicitor in great detail and before reaching a financial agreement.

The advantage of judicial separation proceedings as opposed to divorce proceedings is that in the event of the death of your spouse you are the widow for pension purposes.

Death-in-service benefit

It is quite common these days for employers to supply their employees with death-in-service benefit. This is a lump-sum payment which usually comprises three times the salary on death. It is payable to the remaining spouse and/or children if the employee dies while he or she is still employed by the company. Most companies appoint trustees to administer the fund and each employee is requested to nominate a person or persons to whom the fund should be distributed on his or her death. It is usual for an employee to nominate his wife as the beneficiary of the fund in the event of his death. If the employee gets divorced, or even more appropriately if he or she remarries, the death-in-service benefit nomination may be transferred to a second wife or all subsequent children. Again, you should take into consideration a death-in-service benefit, if this is available, in any financial settlement. It is usual to request an undertaking from the employee to nominate, say one half or even the whole of the death-in-service benefit either to the first wife or solely to the children of the family.

Insurance policies

Most couples will have taken out life insurance, and often they will have a number of additional insurance policies for various different reasons. For example, if your spouse is self-employed there may be insurance policies specifically allotted to pension arrangements. Insurance policies and their surrender value should be taken into consideration in any financial settlement. Many couples have policies which are taken out by the husband on his life and written for the benefit of the wife under the Married Women's Property Act (1882). You must decide what is to be done with these policies. It may be necessary for the benefit to be assigned elsewhere. Policies which are in joint name must also be considered. These will be transferred to one spouse or the other as part of the financial settlement.

Education
School fees
A parent who is separated or divorced may pay school fees as part of a child's maintenance and thereby, in effect, obtain tax relief on the payment. However, this depends upon the agreement of the school to enter into a form of contract with the child which is acceptable to the Inland Revenue. The Inland Revenue have produced a form of contract which should be used in all cases. The contract is signed by the bursar of the school (or the headmaster) and the child. The parent signs a separate deed of indemnity relating to the school fees, in order to satisfy the school that the fees will be paid.

The form of the court order dealing with the child's maintenance and the school fees must be prepared in a way which makes it acceptable to the Inland Revenue, as follows:

> The respondent do pay or cause to be paid to the child of the family as from 1st January 1986 for so long as he/she shall continue to receive full time education or further order, periodical payments for herself:
> (a) Of an amount equivalent to such sums as after deduction of income tax at the basic rate equals the school fees including specified extras at the educational establishment from time to time attended by him/her during each financial year payable termly together with,
> (b) The sum of £xxx per month less tax in respect of his/her general maintenance.

It is not possible for you to obtain tax relief on the payment of school fees if the children concerned are living with you and are, in effect, in your care and control.

If your solicitor does believe that you will be able to obtain tax relief on school fees, he or she should enquire at your child's school to see if it is prepared to enter into this form of contract. Some schools will not enter into a contract with the child. In these cases, the amount of the school fees can be added to the sum for the child's general maintenance and a court order obtained for the total sum. The money which is paid to the child in this way must be administered carefully and the payment in respect of the school fees must be made into a special bank account which the parent who has care and control holds specifically for the child. This parent must then enter into an agreement with the school to pay the fees from this account. In this sort of order the amount of the school fees is added to the sum for general maintenance and so the child may well have to pay tax on the maintenance payment.

The alternative may be to pay the school fees either to the child under a general maintenance order, or to your spouse on the undertaking that the fees will be paid from this sum of money. In this way, tax relief can still be achieved. However, check the precise figures with your solicitor to ensure that this method is viable. Remember that any monies paid to your child over £2,335 a year for the tax year 1986/87 will be taxed, as will any monies paid to your spouse over £3,655 a year for the tax year 1986/87 if he or she has dependent children.

[The case of *Sherdley v Sherdley* may lead to a change in the Inland Revenue practice of allowing divorced or separated parents to obtain tax relief on school fees. The matter is, at present, under consideration and you should check the situation with your solicitor.]

University grants

A child who is resident with a parent whose income is below that of its other parent may put forward the income of the parent with whom he or she resides for grant assessment purposes. Any income which the child receives (for example, maintenance) will be taken into consideration when assessing the amount of the educational grant. Any reduction in the grant is usually a reduction pound for pound. Make sure that your child (or you) looks into the assessment of income before applying for a university grant. For further information you should contact the enquiries office of your local education department.

Wills

A will is not automatically revoked by a decree of divorce. However, so far as an ex-spouse is concerned he or she will be treated as if he or she died the day before the final decree of divorce, *divorce absolute*. So any gift or monies left to that ex-spouse will pass to the person who is entitled to the residue of the estate. If the divorced person has not made a will and the estate therefore passes under the intestacy rule, an ex-spouse will receive no benefit. This provision will not affect any children of the marriage named as beneficiaries in the will.

It is always advisable to make a fresh will at the commencement of divorce proceedings so as to avoid any possible complication in the future.

Remember that remarriage will automatically revoke a current will and therefore if you remarry you should make a fresh will or re-execute a copy of your current will. A will is not affected by a decree of divorce in Scotland and Northern Ireland.

Chapter 8

The unmarried couple

More and more people are deciding to live together rather than to marry. Family law is based on the legal rights and duties which arise on marriage and people who live together without marriage do not have those rights and duties. Marriage is the main basis of English society, but as more people live together, there has been an increase in the recognition of cohabitation as a status within society. It is a commonly held view that to live together as a common law husband and wife confers the same rights upon those parties as living together as husband and wife, lawfully married. This is not so. In fact the phrases common law husband and common law wife have no legal meaning.

Ownership of property

The ownership of a house is always an important issue in the breakdown of a relationship whether married or unmarried. In the case of an unmarried couple, the question of ownership will depend upon whose name appears upon the title documents of the property.

Joint ownership

If you have purchased a property with another person with whom you have a relationship and that property has been placed in your joint names, then when the relationship breaks down, the property will normally be held between you as joint beneficial owners in equal shares. This means that after the repayment or deduction of the outstanding mortgage, the balance is normally divided between you and your partner equally. If one person has contributed more money than the other (for example, one of you might have put down a £5,000 deposit while the other might have contributed nothing in the way of direct cash) then you should lodge a statement signed by both of you, with the title deeds to show the proportional interest each of you hold in the house. It is desirable to consider the position at the outset and record in writing what are the intentions of the joint owners as to the shares.

Example 8

John and Mary purchased a flat in their joint names for £32,000. John had inherited £5,000 from an uncle and agreed that this should be put into the property. John and Mary then obtained a mortgage for £27,000 and the property was placed in their joint names. If there had been no statement attached to the deeds, on sale of the property John and Mary would each have been entitled to one half of the equity of the property. However, it had been agreed that John's £5,000 would be reflected in their respective shares in the property, so John got this sum back when the property was eventually sold for £40,000. The mortgage of £27,000 was repaid, £5,000 was paid to John and the balance was divided equally between them, which amounted to £4,000 each. They agreed that John would withdraw the sum of £5,000 rather than expressing this as a percentage of the sale proceeds but the latter, of course, can be agreed if you prefer.

Sole name

Many people have encountered problems in a situation where one party purchases the property in his or her sole name and a girlfriend or boyfriend moves into the property at a later date. The relationship is seen as a stable, long-term relationship but the purchaser does not bother to change the legal ownership of the house. When this sort of relationship breaks up, the party without ownership will have no right to a lump sum, or to any part of the share of the proceeds of the sale of the house merely on account of the fact that he or she has been in a relationship for some period of time, and has contributed to the upkeep of the property. It often seems unfair that someone who has improved a property by spending money on furnishings, decoration and so on will, at the end of the relationship (and in the absence of agreement) find that he or she cannot claim financial compensation through the court for this expenditure.

In some cases, it is possible for the party, whose name is not on the title document, to establish a beneficial interest in the property by proving that the other party holds the property on trust for them both. However, this is difficult unless one party has obviously contributed towards the purchase of the property – there must be a direct financial contribution towards the purchase price either when the property is bought or by putting in a lump sum to reduce the mortgage (and if possible putting a letter on the title deed explaining the situation). This is because of the much wider powers given to the courts in recent years dealing with married people. People who live together without being married have only their strict property rights which cannot be adjusted by the court. If a trust can be established, then the parties will normally have an interest in the property equivalent to the financial contribution made. Taking the example of Mary and John, if Mary contributed three quarters and the property was bought in his name, then John would hold the property on trust for Mary at one quarter of its value after deduction of the mortgage. Mortgage repayments have been considered by the court to count as a contribution towards the purchase price. Similarly, physical work which improves the structure of the property may also be regarded as a direct contribution towards the purchase of the property.

One of the advantages of cohabitation is that unmarried parties can each claim tax relief on mortgage interest up to £30,000 respectively. So, if the home is in their joint names, and they have a joint mortgage, they will receive tax relief on the interest on a loan of up to £60,000.

Supplementary benefit

An unmarried couple who are living together as husband and wife would have no supplementary benefit advantages because their requirements and resources are aggregated for supplementary benefit purposes. For further information with regard to supplementary benefit you should contact your local branch of the DHSS.

Maintenance

A cohabitee has no statutory right to be maintained by the other cohabitee. On separation, there is no procedure whereby a female cohabitee can request and enforce a claim to be maintained by the male cohabitee, nor vice versa.

If the couple have children, an affiliation order (an application for maintenance of an illegitimate child) can be obtained against the father of the child and the father can obtain tax relief in respect of that court order. (If circumstances are appropriate, the father, too, can apply for an affiliation order against the mother for maintenance for the child.) However, a maintenance application must be made to the court within three years of the birth of the child (unless it can be proved to the court that the father has in fact paid some maintenance to the child at some point within the first three years of its life). In these proceedings, the mother must prove her allegation of paternity and the court has the power to insist that blood tests are obtained. In this way, a child can be maintained by its father until it reaches school leaving age, or later, if the court specifically makes such an order.

It is important to remember that if you decide to cohabit, rather than to marry, that the rights and duties imposed by formal marriage do not pertain to cohabitation. If, when cohabitees separate, no private agreement can be reached between the two, the options for maintenance and support of each individual and/or any children of the family are substantially curtailed.

The Inheritance (Provision for Family and Dependants) Act (1975)

This act provides for applications to be made to the court that maintenance to a person should be continued after one party's death if, at the time of that party's death, he or she was maintaining the other person as a dependant. The act also applies to an illegitimate child who has the same rights on the intestacy of his father and mother as a legitimate child. If, for example, the father has made a will excluding the illegitimate child, but that child is being maintained by the father at the time of the father's death, the illegitimate child has a right to apply to the court for the maintenance to continue – provided there are sufficient funds to make this feasible.

Chapter 9

Coping with legal costs

Solicitors charge on a time basis. Each solicitor will have an hourly rate at which he or she works and at the outset you should ask your solicitor his or her rate and a rough estimate of the cost of your case. It is extremely difficult for a solicitor to give an accurate estimate of the cost of a case because it depends entirely on how much work that solicitor is going to do, and that in turn depends largely on the attitude that your spouse and/or his or her solicitor are going to take to the matter in hand. So, ask your solicitor for a regular account of costs so that you know how much you are spending as you go along. It usually helps to pay your solicitor's account on a regular basis, for example every three months, so you do not get landed with a large bill at the end of the day which you will find more difficult to settle. Most solicitors will ask you for a payment on account of cost at the beginning of the case. This payment can vary from £100 to £1,000, or more, depending on the complexity of the case and the policy of that particular firm.

The legal process can be an expensive business and you should be aware of this throughout your case. With this in mind, and conscious of the fact that the legal costs are often paid with money from the family pool, many family solicitors encourage their clients to reach an amicable agreement if this is at all possible. It is often unnecessary to build up enormous legal costs (often thousands of pounds) when the money could be used for the benefit of the family. This is usually a more productive use for the money than fighting with your spouse on a question of principle.

A solicitor's hourly rate may range from as low as £25.00 per hour to £100.00 per hour or more. When you receive your final bill, many solicitors who charge at the lower end of the scale may have inserted a percentage increase for skill, care and attention. This, of course, will have the effect of a higher hourly charging rate. When you first contact a solicitor, ask for the charging rate, enquire whether in addition to that hourly figure, there is a percentage increase at the end of the day, whether there is an extra for letters received and letters written, and whether there are any other extra charges you may incur. You should also remember that VAT is charged on all solicitors' costs and disbursements (unless you are resident abroad for tax purposes).

Court fees are added to a solicitor's bill. There is a court fee of £40.00 on filing a petition and there is also a court fee of £10.00 on the issue of every summons and on the application to make *decree nisi* absolute. If you attend court, for example, for your financial hearing and you spend a day there, you do not pay for the use of the court or for the judge's time but you will pay for your solicitor's time in attending court with you and for your barrister, if one has been instructed to represent you. Again, if you are going to use a barrister, you should ask your solicitor to give you some idea of the barrister's fees.

Please remember that solicitors charge on a time basis. If you spend 20 minutes chatting to your solicitor on the telephone you will be charged for 20 minutes of his or her time. Try and keep your telephone calls brief and to the point; it is much better to write to your solicitor clearly setting out your views and/or instructions than to get involved in a rambling telephone conversation. Bear in mind that every minute your solicitor spends on your case, must be paid for by you.

Most importantly, make sure that at the outset you discuss with your solicitor his charging rate and the method of payment.

Taxation of a bill

You are entitled to a detailed account from your solicitor and if you have any questions or queries you should raise them as soon as you can. If you consider that your solicitor's bill is too high, then you are entitled (where there have been no court proceedings) to have the bill look at by the Law Society who will make a final decision. If there have been court proceedings (which would be usual in the context of divorce) and you disagree with your solicitor's account to you, you are entitled to have your account 'taxed' by the court. When this happens, a registrar looks at your solicitor's bill, together with the file of papers, and decides whether or not you have been overcharged.

It is also quite common, when a financial agreement has been reached between parties, that an order is made that one party should settle the other party's legal costs 'to be taxed if not agreed'. This is most common where the husband has agreed to pay the wife's legal costs. If this is the case, the husband is entitled to look at his wife's solicitor's detailed account and if he considers that it is too high he is entitled to ask the court to check the account. This checking procedure is called the 'taxation of a bill'. It is a rather misleading term and has nothing to do with the Inland Revenue.

Legal aid

Each year the government allots a sum of money to the legal aid fund which is administered by the Law Society. The legal aid fund is available to help pay for your solicitor's legal charges in respect of your case. However, in matrimonial disputes, it is very often the case that legal aid serves as a cash flow solution rather than an actual payment. The most important fact to remember about legal aid is that any financial help you do receive will be recovered from any money or property worth more than £2,500 which you retain or obtain as a result of the divorce proceedings (refer to the statutory charge). Ultimately, you may well end up paying your solicitor's costs in total.

There are three types of legal aid that can be given:

1 Legal advice and assistance (the green form scheme)

If you qualify for 'green form advice' from your solicitor, it means that he or she will be covered for the cost of an initial consultation giving general advice about your case, writing letters, making telephone calls, doing a certain amount of negotiation and perhaps obtaining a barrister's opinion. Green form assistance will also cover the preparation and filing of a petition for divorce.

In order to obtain advice and assistance under the green form scheme, you must be able to show that you qualify financially. You may be asked to pay a contribution out of your savings or income and your solicitor at the first consultation will calculate that contribution. Your solicitor will normally ask you to pay the contribution immediately but if you are unable to do so, he or she may accept the payment by instalments. If your contribution turns out to be more than your solicitor's bill, then the balance will be refunded to you.

To establish whether or not you are eligible for green form advice, your disposable capital and disposable income must be calculated. In calculating your disposable capital the following will be disregarded:

(a) The value of the main or only dwelling house in which you reside;
(b) The value of household furniture and effects, articles of personal clothing and tools of your trade;
(c) The subject matter of the advice and assistance from your solicitor.

The maximum disposable capital allowed is as follows:
* £800.00 – client with no dependants;
* £1,000 – client with one dependant;

* £1,120 – client with two dependants.
Add £60 for each additional dependant. When calculating disposable income you should deduct:

(a) Income tax;
(b) Social security payments;
(c) £29.06 in respect of either a husband or wife if you are living together and where you are already separated or even divorced, the allowance will be the actual maintenance paid by you in the last seven days;
(d) £12.75 for each dependent child under 11 years of age.
£19.13 for each dependent child over 11 years but under 16 years of age;
£23.00 for each dependent child or dependent relative of 16 and 17 years of age;
£29.81 for each dependent child of 18 years of age or over.

Your contribution towards your legal aid

Disposable in £ (it must not exceed this figure per week)	£
54	nil
62	5
67	11
71	16
75	21
79	25
83	29
87	34
91	38
95	42
99	47
104	52
108	57
114	62

Thus, you qualify for legal advice and assistance if your disposable income is £114 per week or less and your disposable capital is £800 or less.

2 Assistance by way of representation

You may apply for assistance by way of representation through your solicitor if it is necessary for your solicitor to prepare your case and to represent you in most civil cases in the magistrates courts. These cases can include separation, maintenance, custody and affiliation. Your solicitor will ask you to fill in a green form together with another form and the legal aid officer will assess whether or not it is reasonable for you to be granted assistance by way of representation. The same income conditions apply for assistance by way of representation as for legal advice and assistance under the green form scheme.

With regard to capital, the maximum disposable capital for financial eligibility for assistance by way of representation is as follows:
* £3,000 – client with no dependants
* £3,200 – client with one dependant
* £3,320 – client with two dependants

Add £60 for each additional dependant.

If you have already paid a contribution under the legal aid advice and assistance scheme with regard to the same problem for which you now need representation in court, that contribution will count towards your maximum contribution.

3 Civil legal aid – the full legal aid certificate

A civil legal aid certificate is available to cover all work in negotiating and preparing court proceedings including representation by a solicitor and if necessary, a barrister. A civil legal aid certificate is available for cases in all civil courts, ie the county court, the magistrates court, the high court, the court of appeal and the House of Lords.

A full legal aid certificate is available only if court proceedings are about to be or have been instituted. In most cases of separation and divorce this would require the filing of a divorce petition. Legal aid is not available to pay for the costs of undefended divorce proceedings themselves but is available to cover the costs of the financial application and custody, care and control, and access proceedings within an undefended divorce. Legal aid is available for defended divorce proceedings but the Law Society applies strict criteria to the grant of a legal aid certificate for a defended divorce and must be satisfied that there is a legitimate case to answer.

Emergency legal aid

An application for emergency legal aid can be made for emergency cases such as applications for maintenance and for wardship proceedings. The application is made on a pink form and at the same time an application is made for a full civil legal aid certificate. If you turn out not to qualify for legal aid, when your means have been assessed fully you will have to pay the legal costs yourself which you incurred under the emergency certificate.

However, it is quite possible for your solicitor to start preliminary negotiations, which may lead to a settlement, under the green form scheme if you are eligible.

You must qualify financially before a civil legal aid certificate can be granted. You must also show that you have reasonable grounds for commencing proceedings and that your case has merit. Your solicitor will do an initial calculation as to your qualifications for legal aid and if he or she considers that you are within the financial limit you will be asked to complete the appropriate application form. The form will contain a brief statement about the nature of your case to enable the Law Society who administers the legal aid fund to assess whether or not your application should proceed. Once your application has been accepted, the local office of the DHSS will be asked to assess in more detail your financial position and you will receive correspondence from the DHSS and further forms to complete. You should ensure that you complete and return all forms sent to you from the DHSS as soon as possible, and as accurately as possible. It takes approximately six to eight weeks to process a legal aid application and it is possible that very little can be done on your case before the grant of a full legal aid certificate, even if you are in receipt of green form advice. Delay in returning the appropriate forms or carelessness when completing the forms may lead to further delay.

Financial qualifications

Your disposable income will be calculated by assessing your income for the following 12 months and deducting from that income the following items:
* Income tax
* National insurance
* Superannuation
* Pension contributions
* Employment expenses ie fares to work, trade union membership, and child care where reasonable
* Rent and rates (less rebates)
* Mortgage repayments
* Allowances for family and dependants.

Allowances for family and dependants

	Yearly in £	Weekly in £
Spouse	1,511	29.06
Dependent children		
Under 11	663	12.75
Between 11 and 15	995	19.13
Between 16 and 17	1,196	23.00
18 and over	1,550	29.81

Having made all these deductions, what is left is your disposable income. If your disposable income is £5,415 per annum or less, you will qualify for legal aid.

If your disposable income is £2,255 or less you will pay no contribution towards your legal costs. If your disposable income is between £2,255 and £5,415 you will have to pay towards the cost of your case from your income. The contribution will be a quarter of your disposable income. If you receive an offer of legal aid and that offer is accepted by you, any contribution from savings should be paid straight away. Any contribution from income is normally paid by 12 monthly instalments and you will be issued with a paying-in book.

Disposable capital includes the following:

* Cash savings
* Bank or national savings bank accounts
* National savings certificates
* Premium saving bonds
* Money in building society accounts
* Money that can be borrowed against a surrender value of any life insurance or endowment policy
* Anything of substantial value such as shares, jewellery, antiques
* Value of any property other than that property in which you live.

The following are disregarded for the purposes of calculating disposable capital:

* The value of the house in which you live
* Your furniture and fittings and clothes and any tools of your trade
* The value of the matter in dispute.

If your disposable capital is £4,710 or less you will qualify for civil legal aid. Even if your disposable capital is more than £4,710, you may still be offered a civil legal aid certificate if your case is likely to be expensive.

If your disposable capital is £3,000 or less you will not have to pay a contribution. If your savings are more than £3,000 you will have to pay a contribution and it is likely that you will have to pay this at once. The maximum that you will be asked to pay is all your disposable capital over £3,000 but it may very well be less.

If at any time your financial situation changes you should inform your solicitor and the legal aid office and you will be re-assessed. It may be helpful to obtain a *Legal Aid Guide* from the head office or from your local legal aid office (see Appendix A).

Legal aid in Scotland and Northern Ireland

There are similar legal aid schemes in Scotland and Northern Ireland. For further information on the situation in Scotland, contact the Legal Aid Central Committee at the Law Society of Scotland (see Appendix A). For information on the situation in Northern Ireland, contact the Legal Aid Department at the Incorporated Law Society of Northern Ireland (see Appendix A).

Legal aid for representation abroad

Many countries have legal aid schemes and you should ask your solicitor to make further enquiries at the Legal Aid Head Office (see Appendix F).

The statutory charge

When you apply for a legal aid certificate your solicitor will give a written explanation of the workings of the statutory charge. You should read this explanation very carefully and if you have any questions or queries relating to it, ask your solicitor immediately. There is often considerable misunderstanding about the meaning of and the working of the statutory charge.

The purpose of the statutory charge is to recoup some of the monies expended by the legal aid fund on costs. The legal aid statutory charge is a charge by the Legal Aid Fund on property involved in the proceeding which is recovered or preserved. In matrimonial proceedings there is an exemption for the first £2,500 of property which has been recovered or preserved. However, the property you receive in excess of that value you will contribute to your legal aid costs.

If you do not understand this at the outset of your case, you may continue to litigate, quite possibly unnecessarily, believing that you will not have to pay your solicitor's costs. It can come as a nasty shock to discover that, for example, a lump sum payment rewarded to you by the court of £15,000 has been swallowed up by your legal costs, save for the £2,500 exemption.

If the final settlement of your divorce has been on a cash basis then that money must be paid to your solicitor and your solicitor is under a duty to retain sufficient funds to cover his costs. This is accounted for to the Law Society Legal Aid Office, who will take into account any contribution which you may already have made towards your solicitor's costs. Once the amount of the solicitor's bill has been settled by the Law Society, you will receive any balance of the settlement monies which may be due to you. Your solicitor will account directly to the Law Society for the monies which you owe to the Legal Aid Fund in respect of your legal costs under the working of the statutory charge.

If you have recovered property in the form of the matrimonial home then the Law Society has a right to a charge over the property rather like a second mortgage. At present, the Law Society does not charge interest upon this amount. Suppose that the matrimonial home was in joint names and that the court ordered, by way of a financial settlement, that one party's share of the equity of the matrimonial home should be transferred outright to the other party. The latter would then own the whole of the equity in the matrimonial home which is valued at £50,000. The recipient, who used to own £25,000 worth of equity now owns £50,000 worth of equity. The first £2,500 of monies which he or she has recovered or preserved is exempt, but the Law Society has a claim for £3,500 of solicitor's costs on the monies which were recovered or preserved. However, the monies are tied up in the property which cannot be sold because it is needed to house the children. In this sort of case, the Law Society will register a charge on the property which will come behind the mortgage. Where there is a mortgage on the property of £10,000, for example, the title deeds will then show the Law Society's charge for £3,500 which represents solicitor's costs. When the owner eventually sells the property he, or she will be required to repay not only the mortgage but also £3,500 to the Law Society.

It is a matter of debate as to whether property has been recovered and preserved or not. The Law Society has produced a very useful booklet entitled *Civil Legal Aid (Understanding The Statutory Charge)* which can be obtained from the Legal Aid Head Office (see Appendix F).

Orders for costs in court proceedings

All court proceedings involve costs; at the end of each court appearance it rests with the court to decide who is to pay the costs of the proceedings.

Divorce proceedings

It is usual, in the case of a divorce based on adultery, for the petitioner to ask in the petition for an order that the respondent and co-respondent pay the petitioner's costs. This may also occur in the case of an unreasonable behaviour and desertion petition. An order for costs in these cases can be made at the time of the pronouncement of *decree nisi* and it is up to the petitioner to enforce that order. The costs of the divorce proceedings themselves are usually in the region of £200. In the case of a petition based on two years' separation, it is considered that both parties agreed to the decree of divorce and as such one party should not be asked to bear the other party's costs.

Financial proceedings

The costs accumulated during financial proceedings can be considerable, especially where one party refuses or fails adequately to disclose his financial position, thus creating extra work and investigation for the other spouse's solicitor. In this sort of situation, it is likely that an order for costs will be made against that spouse. The object of an order for costs is to compensate one party as opposed to penalising the 'loser'.

The question of costs of proceedings and a court hearing can sometimes be dealt with if one party has written to the other party a letter of offer of settlement based on the principal in *Calderbank v Calderbank*. This is known as a Calderbank letter and is written 'without prejudice' and therefore its contents are not to be revealed to the court without the consent of both parties. However, the party on whose behalf the letter was written reserves the right to raise the letter with regard to the question of costs, if the offer in the letter is not accepted by the other party and, at a subsequent hearing the court makes an order similar to the offer made in the letter. On that basis the court can order one party to pay the other party's costs from the date of the letter to the conclusion of the court hearing, if the offer in the letter was in terms the same as or better than the order of the court.

So, if your solicitor receives an offer of settlement in your case in terms of a Calderbank letter, consider it carefully and listen to your solicitor's advice.

Custody and access proceedings

It is unusual for an order for costs to be made against one party in custody and access proceedings unless that party's behaviour has been excessively obstructive and unreasonable.

The terms

An order for costs may be made in the following terms:

(a) Party and party costs: the costs incurred by solicitors corresponding with each other, speaking on the telephone, drafting the recessing documents for the proceedings;
(b) Solicitor and own client costs: all the costs of conducting your case;
(c) Common fund costs: the costs charged by the solicitor to the legal aid fund for work done on your case.

Are you entitled to state benefits?

It is possible that you may be entitled to supplementary benefit or Family Income Supplement if the separation or subsequent divorce leaves you in such a difficult financial position as to make you eligible for such help.

Supplementary benefit

You will qualify for supplementary benefit if:
1 You have capital or savings not more than £3,000;
2 You come within the scale rate for income. This depends on whether you are married or separated and on the number of children. The scale rate is calculated to cover day-to-day expenses;

3 You work no longer than 30 hours a week. If you are unemployed you must register available for work, although if you are a single parent with a dependent child under 16 years who is living with you, you can claim benefit without registering yourself as available for work.

You can claim supplementary benefit from your local DHSS. In exceptional cases, a single sum payment can be given but this depends on your own savings position. Housing benefit, help with rent or rates, is available to those who qualify.

Family income supplement

Family income supplement is payable to a family with at least one dependent child under the age of 16 years or 19 years if he or she is still in full-time education. This benefit is payable to families on low incomes. Where there is a single parent who works for 24 hours or more a week, on a low income and with at least one dependent child, family income supplement can be claimed. Again, the claim is made to the DHSS.

There are approximately 60 different cash benefits available from your local social security office. It is worth finding out if you qualify for any of these. The DHSS produces a useful booklet, *Which Benefit? Sixty Ways to Get Cash Help*, which is available from their Leaflets Unit (see Appendix A). The pamphlet covers information on the following benefits and many others:

Supplementary benefit
Family income supplement
Housing benefit
Rate rebate
Free NHS dental treatment
Free glasses and prescription
Free milk and vitamins
Maternity grant and maternity allowance
Child benefit
Single parent benefit
Free school meals, milk, fares to school, uniform and clothing grant
Educational maintenance allowance
Unemployment benefit
Sickness benefit
Industrial injury benefit
War disablement pensions
Criminal injuries compensation
Attendance allowance for the disabled
Invalid care allowance

Mobility allowance
Retirement pension details
Widow's allowance

The DHS leaflet FB3 – *Help for one parent families* is very useful as is *The Supplementary Benefits Handbook*.

Child benefit is paid for every child of the family and stands at £7.10 per week per child. Single parent benefit can be paid to a separated parent with a dependent child once the parent has been separated from his or her spouse for a period of 13 weeks. Single parent benefit is £4.60 per week.

Your local Citizen's Advice Bureau will be able to give you further advice on the subject of state benefits. DHSS offices provide information but they are often extremely busy and it may be difficult for them to find the time to explain the benefits to you.

Chapter 10

Scotland and Ireland

Divorce proceedings in Scotland and Northern Ireland
The procedure which has been discussed in this book relates only to England and Wales. The jurisdiction of the family law does not relate to the whole of the United Kingdom and there are quite considerable differences in practice, procedure and terminology in Scotland and Northern Ireland.

Scotland
In Scotland, a petition for divorce can be presented at any time after the marriage (whereas in England the marriage must have lasted for at least one year before the presentation of the petition for divorce to the court).

There is only one decree of divorce and no equivalent, in Scotland, of the English *decree nisi*, the first decree of divorce. In England the statutory period of six weeks between *decree nisi* and *decree absolute* gives a period for reflection and possible reconciliation. In Scotland there is no such period, although a decree can be appealed within 21 days of being granted.

The irretrievable breakdown of the marriage ground for divorce is the same in Scotland as in England and the facts upon which that ground must be proved are also the same. However, the person who seeks the divorce is called the pursuer while the other person is the defender.

Scotland does have a 'speedy' procedure for divorce where there are no children of the marriage or at least none under the age of 16 years and where neither party is making financial claims against the other. In these circumstances, a couple may obtain a decree of divorce on the basis that they have been separated for a period of two years (with the consent of each other's spouse) or a period of five years without both spouses' consent. The appropriate printed form can be obtained from the court and the procedure is comparatively simple and very similar to the English divorce procedure.

Where there are children under the age of 16 years and/or one spouse is making financial claims, the procedure is a little more complicated. In these circumstances, you would be well advised to consult a solicitor.

The procedure

A summons is lodged in court by the pursuer and served upon the defender. If the case is to be a defended divorce, the defender must indicate his or her intentions to the court and lodge a defence. The case will ultimately proceed to a hearing.

If the case is to be undefended, the pursuer and a supporting witness will swear affidavits which are lodged in the court and if the judge is satisfied with the contents of the affidavits, a decree of divorce will be pronounced.

The pursuer's affidavit must deal with the arrangements for the children and disclose the financial position of both parties so far as they are known to the pursuer.

The one major difference between the Scottish and English system is that where there are children involved an affidavit must be lodged by a person who is not the pursuer or the defender. The affidavit must deal with the accommodation and general welfare of the children and it is usually sworn by a close relative or neighbour.

If the proceedings are undefended, it will not be necessary for the pursuer to appear in court and a decree of divorce will be pronounced. Again, this differs from the English procedure which demands that where children are involved, there must always be at least one attendance before a judge to satisfy the judge as to the arrangements for the children. In Scotland, the judge can certify that he is satisfied with the arrangement by virtue of reading the affidavits only and neither the mother nor the father need appear.

Legal aid is available in Scotland for divorce proceedings, although the system differs from the one which exists in England and Wales. The Legal Aid Central Committee at the Law Society of Scotland (see Appendix A) will provide you with a leaflet entitled *Guide to Legal Aid in Scotland*.

Finance

Maintenance in Scotland is known as the 'periodical allowance' and maintenance for children is called 'aliment'. The court is empowered to order a capital payment but application for this payment must be made before the decree of divorce has been pronounced. Tax relief is available on maintenance payments made under a court order.

Aliment can be paid under the 'huggings' formula which can substantially reduce the payment of tax. In this way, payments are made to the parent with custody of the children, in trust for the children and this payment will be deemed to be the child's income to be set against the child's personal allowance for tax purposes.

The position in Northern Ireland

The Matrimonial Causes (Northern Ireland) Order (1978) is the piece of legislation which principally governs divorce proceedings in Northern Ireland. The law and the procedure is, in general, the same as in England and Wales. The main difference is that in order to obtain a decree of divorce in Northern Ireland the parties must attend the court and give their evidence to the judge in person, as opposed to relying on affidavit evidence under special procedure in England and Wales.

Appendix A

List of useful addresses

Alcoholics Anonymous
PO Box 514
11 Redcliffe Gardens
London SW10 9BQ
Tel 01-352 9779

DHSS Leaflets Unit
PO Box 21
Stanmore
Middlesex HA7 1AY

DHSS (Public Enquiries Office)
Alexander Fleming House
Elephant and Castle
London SE1

Families Need Fathers
37 Carden Road
London SE15

Family Forum
Cambridge House
131 Camberwell Road
London SE5 0HF

Gingerbread
35 Wellington Street
London WC2

(The) Incorporated Law Society of Northern Ireland
Bedford House
16–22 Bedford Street
Belfast BT2 7FL
Tel 0232 246 441

Inland Revenue (Public Enquiries Room)
West Wing
Somerset House
Strand
London WC2 1LB
Tel 01-438 6420

Jewish Family Mediation Service
3 Gower Street
Bloomsbury
London WC1
Tel 01-636 9380

Land Charges Department
Burngate Way
Plymouth PL5 3LP

Land Registry
Lincoln's Inn Fields
London WC2A 3PH

(The) Law Society
113 Chancery Lane
London WC2
Tel 01-242 1222

(The) Law Society of Scotland
PO Box 123
41–43 Drumsheugh Gardens
Edinburgh EH3 7SW
Tel 031 226 7061

London Jewish Marriage Council
23 Ravenshurst Avenue
London NW4
Tel 01-203 6311

Mothers Apart From Their Children (MATCH)
64 Delaware Mansions
Delaware Road
London W9

National Association of Citizens' Advice Bureaux
115 Pentonville Road
London N1

National Council for the Divorced and Separated
41 Summit Avenue
Kingsbury
London NW9

National Council for One Parent Families
255 Kentish Town Road
London NW5 2LX
Tel 01-267 1361

National Family Conciliation Council
34 Milton Road
Swindon
Wiltshire SN1 5JH

(The) National Fostercare Association
Francis House
Francis Street
London SW1P 1DE

National Marriage Guidance Council
Herbert Grey College
Little Church Street
Rugby CV21 3AP

Scottish Council for Single Parents
13 Gayfield Square
Edinburgh

Solicitors' Family Law Association
154 Fleet Street
London EC4A 2HX
Secretary: P H Grose-Hodge

Stepfamily (National Stepfamily Association)
Room 3
Ross Street Community Centre
Ross Street
Cambridge CB1 3BS

Women's Aid Federation
Tel 01-837 9316

Appendix B

Solicitors' Family Law Association Code of Practice

The Association recommends that members and any solicitor practising family law should adopt the following code of practice.

General

1.1 The solicitor should endeavour to advise, negotiate and conduct proceedings in a manner calculated to encourage and assist the parties to reconcile their differences and should inform the client of the approach he intends to adopt.

1.2 The solicitor should encourage the client to see the advantage to the family of a conciliatory rather than a litigious approach as a way of resolving the disputes. The solicitor should explain to the client that in nearly every case where there are children, the attitude of the client to the other party in any negotiations will affect the family as a whole and may affect the relationship of the children with the parents.

1.3 The solicitor should encourage the attitude that a family dispute is not a contest in which there is one winner and one loser, but rather a search for fair solutions. He should avoid using words or phrases that imply a dispute when no serious dispute necessarily exists, for example, 'opponent', 'win', 'lose', or 'Smith v Smith'.

1.4 Because of the involvement of personal emotions in family disputes the solicitor should where possible avoid heightening such emotions by the advice given; and by avoiding expressing opinions as to the behaviour of the other party.

1.5 The solicitor should also have regard to the impact of correspondence on the other party when writing a letter of which a copy may be sent to that party and should also consider carefully the impact of correspondence on his own client before sending copies of letters to the client.

1.6 The solicitor should aim to avoid or dispel suspicion or mistrust between parties, by encouraging at an early stage where possible, full, frank and clear disclosure of information and openness in dealings.

1.7 The solicitor should aim to achieve settlement of difference as quickly as may be reasonable whilst recognising that the parties may need time to come to terms with their new situation.

Relationship with client

2.1 As a rule the solicitor should explain to the client at the outset the terms of his retainer and take care to ensure that the client is fully aware of the impact of costs on any chosen course of action. The solicitor should thereafter at all stages have regard to the cost of negotiations and proceedings.

2.2 Where appropriate, the solicitor must advise the client of his right to apply for legal aid. He should bear in mind and explain the impact of costs where the client or the other party is in receipt of legal aid, and the particular effect of the statutory charge.

2.3 The solicitor should create and maintain a relationship with his client of a kind which will preserve fully his independent judgement and avoid becoming so involved in the case that his own personal emotions may cloud his judgement.

2.4 Whilst recognising the need to advise firmly and guide the client the solicitor should ensure that where the decision is properly that of the client, it is taken by the client and that its consequences are fully understood, both as to its effect on any children involved and financially.

Dealings with other solicitors

3.1 The solicitor should in all dealings with the other solicitor show courtesy and where possible endeavour to create and maintain a friendly relationship.

3.2 The solicitor should seek wherever possible to foster in his own client a trust in the other party's solicitor, so tending to reduce distrust and suspicion between the parties.

3.3 The solicitor should in financial negotiations make use of without prejudice discussions, that is to say discussions involving conditional offers and conditional admissions that are withdrawn and not disclosed to the court in the event of those negotiations failing. The solicitor should be mindful that an unrealistic offer may be counterproductive and delay settlement.

3.4 The solicitor should generally avoid offering or receiving comments or information 'off the record', where this phrase is intended to mean that the client should not be informed.

Dealings with the other party in person

4.1 In dealings with another party who is not legally represented the solicitor should take particular care to be courteous and restrained. Especial care should be taken to express letters and other communications clearly, avoiding technical language where it is not readily understandable to the layman or might be misunderstood.

4.2 Wherever proceedings are taken or negotiations conducted that may adversely affect the other party's interests, the other party should, in the interests of both parties, be advised to consult a solicitor.

Petitions and proceedings

5.1 The solicitor should avoid allegations or procedures which may cause or increase ill-will between the parties without producing any benefit for the client.

5.2 Before instituting proceedings which make allegations about the other party's conduct, the solicitor should consider whether the other party or his solicitor should be consulted in advance as to the particulars to be alleged or the grounds to be relied on.

5.3 Where the purpose of taking a particular step in proceedings may be misunderstood the solicitor should consider explaining it in advance to the other party or his solicitors.

Children

6.1 The solicitor should treat his work in relation to children as the most important of his duties.

6.2 The solicitor should, in advising, negotiating and conducting proceedings, assist both his client and the other parent to regard the welfare of the child as the first paramount consideration.

6.3 The solicitor should aim to promote cooperation between parents in decisions concerning the child, both by formal arrangements (such as orders for joint custody); by practical arrangements (such as shared involvement in school events) and by consultation on important questions.

6.4 The solicitor must keep in mind that the interests of the child do not necessarily coincide with the interests of either parent, and that occasionally the child should be separately represented. In such case his duty is to bring the matter to the attention of the court.

6.5 The solicitor should take care to keep separate issues of custody and access on the one hand and money on the other. It is often helpful to deal with these two topics in separate letters.

6.6 'Kidnapping' of children both results from and creates exceptional fear, bitterness and desperation in the parents. The solicitor should therefore take what steps he can strongly to discourage kidnapping a child, that is to say, removing a child in breach of an order of a court of any country, or in such a manner to preempt or preclude a decision by the proper court (wherever that court may be) as to the child's custody or access.

The guidelines set out in this Code cannot be absolute rules in as much as the solicitor may have to depart from them if the law or his professional obligations so require. They are a restatement of principles, objectives and recommendations which many solicitors practising family law already seek to follow and to which they seek to aspire in serving their clients.

October 1983

Published with the permission of the Solicitors' Family Law Association.

Appendix C

Sample forms

**Divorce Petition
(Wife against Husband)
(Separation – 2 years)**

MATRIMONIAL
CAUSES RULES   IN THE   COUNTY COURT*
                                          DIVORCE REGISTRY*

Rule 9
Appendix 2
No of matter
The notes for guidance in drafting the petition are on a separate sheet.
The Petition of
Shows that

Note 1.   1. On the   day of   19   the Petitioner was lawfully married to
            (hereinafter called the Respondent) at

Note 2.   2. The Petitioner and the Respondent last lived together as husband and wife at

Note 3.   3. The Petitioner is domiciled in England and Wales
Note 4.   the petitioner is a   and resides at
            and the Respondent is a   and resides at

Note 5.   4. There is (are)   children of the family now living

Note 6.   5. No other child now living has been born to the Petitioner during the marriage

Note 7.

            6. There are or have been no other proceedings in any court in England and Wales or elsewhere with reference to the marriage (or to any children of the family) or between the Petitioner and the Respondent with reference to any
Note 8.   property of either or both of them

122 Appendices

           7. There are no proceedings continuing in any country outside England and Wales which relate to the marriage or are capable of affecting its validity or subsistence.

Note 9.
Note 10.
Note 11.   8. The said marriage has broken down irretrievably.

           9. The parties to the marriage have lived apart for a continuous period of at least two years immediately preceding the presentation of this petition and the Respondent consents to a decree being granted.

Note 13. 10.
Note 14.
Note 15.
Note 16.

           The Petitioner therefore prays:

Note 17. (1) That the said marriage may be dissolved;
Note 18. (2) That she may be granted the custody of

Note 19. (3) That the Respondent   may be ordered to pay   the costs of this suit;
Note 20. (4) That she may be granted the following ancillary relief –
        (i)   an order for maintenance pending suit
        (ii)   a periodical payments order
        (iii) a secured periodical payments order for herself
        (iv) a lump sum order
        (v)   a periodical payments order
        (vi) a secured periodical payments order for the children of the family
        (vii) a lump sum order
        (viii) a property adjustment order
Note 21. (Signed)
Note 22. The names and addresses of the persons who are to be served with this Petition are:
Note 23. The Petitioner's address for service is:
Dated this   day of   19

Address all communications to the Court to: The Registrar, County Court (or to the Divorce Registry, Somerset House, Strand, London WC2R 1LP). The Court Office is open from 10 am till 4 pm (4.30 pm at the Divorce Registry) on Mondays to Fridays only.

In the   County Court*
                    Divorce Registry*

No of matter
IN THE MATTER of the Petitioner of

Divorce Petition
(Wife against Husband)
(Separation – 2 years)

Note 22.

Statement as to arrangements for children

Statement of arrangements
IN THE DIVORCE REGISTRY   No of matter:
Between   Petitioner
and   Respondent

The proposed arrangements for the children of the family under 16 and those over 16 but under 18 who are receiving instruction at an educational establishment or undergoing training for a trade, profession or vocation are as follows:

(i) Residence:

State, in respect of each child, where the child is to live with particulars of the accommodation, what other persons (naming them) live there and who will look after the child; and, if it is proposed that the child should be in the care of a person other than the petitioner, state whether or not that person has agreed to this arrangement.

(ii) Education, etc:

State, in respect of each child, the school or other educational establishment which the child will attend or, if he is working, his place of employment, the nature of his work and details of any training he will receive.

(iii) Financial provision:
State, in respect of each child, who is at present supporting the child or contributing to his support and the extent thereof and whether it is proposed to make any application to the court for the financial support of the child and if so what support is to be applied for.

(iv) Access:
State, in respect of each child, any arrangements which have been agreed for access and the extent to which access is to be given.

The said child/children is/are (not) suffering from serious disability or chronic illness or from the effects of such illness (namely)
State, in respect of each child so suffering, the nature of the disability or illness and attach a copy of any up-to-date medical report which is available.
The said child/children is/are (not) under the care or supervision of a welfare officer, or officer appointed by a local authority or other person or organisation (namely).

Give details and state the date of any order for care and supervision and the circumstances which gave rise to its being made.

Dated this   day of   19   .
This form must be signed by the Petitioner
Signed ....
                                                                            Petitioner
In the County Court
In the Divorce Registry
No of matter:
Between
                                                                            Petitioner
and
                                                                            Respondent
Statement as to arrangements for children
(MCR Form 4)
Rule 8 (2)
Form F907

Acknowledgement of Service

Acknowledgement of Service – Respondent Spouse No.   of

IN THE DIVORCE REGISTRY
IF YOU INTEND TO INSTRUCT A SOLICITOR TO ACT FOR YOU, GIVE HIM THIS FORM IMMEDIATELY
Between   Petitioner
and   Respondent
READ CAREFULLY THIS NOTICE OF PROCEEDINGS BEFORE ANSWERING THE FOLLOWING QUESTIONS
1. Have you received the petition for divorce delivered with this form?
2. On which date and at what address did you receive it?
On the   day of   19
at ....
3. Are you the person named as the Respondent in the petition?
4. Do you intend to defend the case?
5. Do you consent to a decree being granted?
6. In the event of a *decree nisi* being granted on the basis of two years' separation coupled with the respondent's consent, do you intend to apply to the court for it to consider your financial position as it will be after the divorce?
7. Even if you do not intend to defend the case do you object to paying the cost of the proceedings?
If so, on what grounds?
8. Even if you do not intend to defend the case, do you object to the claim in the petition for custody of the children?
9. Do you wish to make any application on your own account for:
(a) custody of the children?
(b) access to the children?
(a) ....
(b) ....
10. *(In the case of proceedings relating to a polygamous marriage)* If you have any wife/husband in addition to the petitioner who is not mentioned in the petition, what is the name and address of each such wife/husband and the date and place of your marriage to her/him?
Dated this   day of   19
If a solicitor is instructed, he will sign opposite on your behalf but if the answer to Question 5 is Yes you must also sign here.
Signed ....
Address
for service ....

Unless you intend to instruct a solicitor, give your place of residence, or if you do not reside in England or Wales, the address of a place in England or Wales to which documents may be sent to you. If you subsequently wish to change your address for service, you must notify the court.
I am/We are acting for the Respondent in this matter.
Signed ....
Address
for service ....

Appendix D

Deed of Separation

This Deed of Separation is made the 1st day of September 1986 Between **JOSEPH JOHN BLOGGS** of 10 Zebra Road, London NW42 (hereinafter called 'the husband') of the one part and **JANE MARY BLOGGS** of 1 Acacia Avenue, London NW43 (hereinafter called 'the wife') of the other part
WHEREAS
(1) the parties were married on the 1st day of January 1978 and there is one child of the family, namely **MARTIN JOSEPH** born on the 30th day of August 1980.
(2) Unhappy differences have arisen between the parties as a result of which they have agreed to live separate and apart from each other from the 19th April 1986.
Now this Deed Witnesseth and it is hereby agreed as follows:
1. The husband and the wife will hereafter live separate and apart as if they were unmarried and each shall be free the other's material control.
2. The husband and the wife will cooperate in the sale of the matrimonial home at 1 Acacia Avenue, London NW43 and will sign all documents and do all things necessary to effect the completion of such sale.
3. The wife shall receive net proceeds of sale of the said matrimonial home to put towards the purchase of a property for herself and the said child of the family, such property to be purchased in the sole name of the wife.
4. The husband will from the 1st day of May 1986 pay or cause to be paid to the wife periodical payments for herself at a rate of £10,000 p.a. less tax payable monthly for joint lives or until further agreement or until an Order of Court is made in her favour.
5. The husband will maintain the said child of the family and will consent to the appropriate orders for periodical payments for the child

and for his school fees (if appropriate) being made in the relevant Court.

6. The said child of the family will remain in the Joint Custody of the parties.

7. The husband and the wife recognise that they have both given careful consideration to the terms of this agreement and accept that this Deed makes fair and reasonable provision for the wife and the said child of the family and that this provision is accepted by the wife in full and final settlement of all the wife's financial claims against the husband (save as to periodical payments).

8. In any subsequent Divorce proceedings the above financial terms will be embodied in an Order of Court in these proceedings and the wife's financial claims against the husband will be dismissed (save as to periodical payments).

9. The husband will pay the wife's reasonable costs in connection with the agreement and execution of this Deed and of any application to an appropriate Court to carry out the terms of paragraph 5 hereof.

SIGNED SEALED AND DELIVERED
by the said JOSEPH JOHN BLOGGS
in the presence of:

SIGNED SEALED AND DELIVERED
by the said JANE MARY BLOGGS
in the presence of:

Appendix E

List of conciliation services affiliated to the National Family Conciliation Council and voluntary organisations associated with conciliation

Birmingham
Birmingham Family Conciliation Service
3 Kingston Row
Birmingham B1 2NU

Bournemouth
Bournemouth and District Family Conciliation Service
2 St Osmund's Road
Parkestone
Poole, Dorset

Bristol
Bristol Courts Family Conciliation Service
Albion Chambers East
Broad Street
Bristol BS1 1DX

Cambridge
Cambridge Family Conciliation Service
2 Pikes Walk, off King Street
Cambridge CB1 1LF

Cardiff
Cardiff Family Conciliation Service
33 Westgate Street
Cardiff

Chelmsford
Mid-Essex Family Conciliation Service
Crown Court Probation Office
New Street
Chelmsford, Essex CM1 1EL

Colchester
North-East Essex Family Conciliation Service
Ryegate House
23 Peter Street
Colchester, Essex CO1 1HL

Coventry
Coventry Family Conciliation Service
Trinity House
33 Trinity Street
Coventry, Warwicks CV1 1FJ

Edinburgh
Scottish Family Conciliation Service (Lothian)
127 Rose Street South Lane
Edinburgh EH2 5BB

Harlow
Harlow and District Family Conciliation Service
Crown Buildings
Crows Road
Epping, Essex CM16 5DA

Ipswich
Ipswich and District Family Conciliation Service
43 Elm Street
Ipswich, Suffolk IPL 2AP

Kent
Kent Family Conciliation Service
The Phoenix Centre
Central Avenue
Sittingbourne, Kent ME10 4BX

Leeds
Leeds Family Conciliation Service
26 Great George Street
Leeds LS1 3DN

London (Central)
Divorce Conciliation and Advisory Service
38 Ebury Street
London SW1W 0LU

London (South-East)
South-East London Family Conciliation Bureau
5 Upper Park Road
Bromley, Kent BR1 3HN

London (South-West)
Mediation in Divorce
51 Sheen Road
Richmond, Surrey TW1 1YG

Middlesbrough
Cleveland Family Conciliation Service
St Mary's Centre
Corporation Road
Middlesbrough, Cleveland

Newcastle
Conciliation Service for Northumberland and Tyneside
MEA House
Ellison Place
Newcastle-upon-Tyne NE1 8XS

Norwich
Norfolk Family Conciliation Service
Charing Cross Centre
17–19 St John Maddermarket
Norwich

North Devon
North Devon Family Conciliation Service
'Court', Alwington
Bideford, North Devon

Reading
Berkshire Family Conciliation Service
1st Floor, 10 Friar's Walk
Friar Street
Reading RG1 1LA

Sheffield
Sheffield Family Conciliation Service
14–18 West Bar Green
Sheffield S1 2DA

Slough
East Berkshire Family Conciliation Service
Law Courts
Slough, Berks SL1 2HJ

Sunderland
Sunderland and South Shields Family Conciliation Service
17 Hillside
Sunderland SR3 1YN

Surrey
Surrey Family Conciliation Service
155 High Street
Dorking, Surrey RH14 1AD

Swindon
Swindon Family Conciliation Service
34 Milton Road
Swindon, Wilts SN1 5JA

Provisionally affiliated and associated services

Bury, Lancs
Family Conciliation Service
c/o National Children's Home Regional Office
33–35 Wilson Patten Street
Warrington, Cheshire WA1 1PG

Bury St Edmunds
Suffolk County Council Western Divisional Office
Shire Hall
Bury St Edmunds
Contact: Mrs Pauline Sefton

Hampshire
Hampshire Family Conciliation Service
11 Beresford Road
Chandler's Ford
Eastleigh SO5 2LU

Harrogate
Harrogate District Family Conciliation Service
1 Haywra Street
Harrogate, Yorks

Hull
Hull and North Humberside Family Conciliation Service
Crown Chambers
Land of Green Ginger
Hull HU1 2PG

London
Institute of Family Therapy Conciliation Service
43 New Cavendish Street
London W1

Ireland
Pilot Family Conciliation Scheme
c/o Drumiskabole
Carraroe
Co Sligo, Eire

Liverpool
Barnardo's Family Conciliation Service
c/o Barnardo's North-West Divisional Office
7 Lineside Close
Liverpool L25 2UD

Middlesex
Middlesex Family Conciliation Service
7c High Street (1st floor)
Barnet, Herts

Northampton
Northampton Family Conciliation Service
8a The Crescent
Plymouth, Devon PL1 3AB

Salisbury
248 St Edmunds Church Street
Salisbury, Wilts SP1 1EF

Scarborough
Scarborough and District Family Mediation Service
12 Falsgrave Road
Scarborough
North Yorkshire YO12 5AT

Somerset
Somerset Family Conciliation Service
37 Chamberlain Street
Wells, Somerset

South Humberside
24 Priestgate
Barton upon Humber
South Humberside DN18 5ET

Sussex
Sussex Family Conciliation Service
22 Stanford Avenue
Brighton, Sussex BN1 6DD

Tunbridge Wells
The Chilston Conciliation Service
St George's Centre
7 Chilston Road
Tunbridge Wells, Kent

York
York Family Mediation Service
Tower House
Fishergate
York YO1 4AU

Appendix F

Legal Aid information

Legal Aid Head Office
Newspaper House
18/16 Great New Street
London EC4V 3BN
Tel 01-353 7411

Legal aid area offices

Birmingham
Podium Centre City House
(Smallbrook Queensway)
5 Hill Street
Birmingham B5 4UD
Tel 021 632 6541

Brighton
9–12 Middle Street
Brighton BN1 1AS
Tel 0273 27003

Bristol
Whitefriars
Middlegate
Lewins Mead
Bristol BS1 2LR
Tel 0272 214 801

Cambridge
Kett House
Station Road
Cambridge CB1 2JT
Tel 0223 66511

Cardiff
Marland House
Central Square
Cardiff CF1 1PF
Tel 0222 388971

Chester
Pepper House
Pepper Row
Chester CH1 1DW
Tel 0244 315455

Leeds
City House
New Station Street
Leeds LS1 4JS
Tel 0532 442851

Liverpool
Moor House
James Street
Liverpool L2 7SA
Tel 051 236 8371

London
29–37 Red Lion Street
London WC1R 4PP
Tel 01-405 6991

Manchester
Pall Mall Court
67 King Street
Manchester M60 9AX
Tel 061 832 7112

Newcastle upon Tyne
Eagle Star House
Fenkle Street
Newcastle upon Tyne NE1 5RU
Tel 032 323461

Nottingham
5 Friar Lane
Nottingham NG1 6BW
Tel 0602 412424

Reading
80 Kings Road
Reading RG1 4LT
Tel 0734 589696

Appendix G

Checklist for income

| **Income per annum** | **Husband** | **Wife** |

Salary net
Benefits from employment

Profits from self employment

State pension
Occupational pension

Interest received:
   Bank
   Building Society
   Other

Dividends etc

Rental income

Trust Income
Payments received under a deed of covenant
Annuities

Other investment income

Social Security
  Child benefit
  Other benefits

Checklist for Expenditure
Regular monthly payments

Property
- Mortgage repayment
- Rental
- Rates
- Water rates
- Gas
- Electricity
- Oil
- Telephone
- Building insurance
- Contents insurance
- Repairs and decoration (house)
- Repairs (electrical and household)

Financial
- Loan repayments
- HP payments
- Credit card payments
- Budget Account
- Life Assurance premiums
- Retirement annuity premiums
- Regular savings plan
- Deed of covenant payments
- Private medical insurance

Living expenses husband and wife
- Housekeeping
- Travel
- Clothing
- Newspapers – magazines
- Tobacco – Drinks
- Cosmetics and toiletries
- Pets

Children
- School fees
- School meals
- Private lessons
- Clothing
- Pocket money
- Sports

Entertainment
- TV Licence
- TV rental
- Meals out
- Family outings
- Books Records
- Sport

Car
- Tax
- Insurance
- Repairs
- Petrol

Subscriptions
- Associations
- Clubs
- Charities

Irregular Payments
- Holidays
- Presents
- Medical
- Tax

Checklist Assets and Liabilities

Assets
- House – current value
- Other real estate
- Cars
- Caravan
- Boat

Shares in own company
Current account in company
Loan account in company
Capital account in business
Bank accounts: current
                deposit
Building Society accounts
National Savings certificates
Premium bonds
Life Assurance policies
Pension plan
Stocks and shares
Interest in trusts

Liabilities
Mortgage on home
Other mortgages
Bank loans
HP debts
Bank overdrafts
Other loans
Credit card balances
Budget account balance
Tax liabilities

Index

Abduction of children, 47–51
Access: access to children, 42–43; access disputes, 46–47; cost of access proceedings, 106
Acknowledgement of service form, 25, 26, 125–126
Addresses: conciliation services, 115, 129–135
general useful addresses, 113–116
Adultery: affidavit requirements, 26
grounds for divorce, 21, 22
six month reconciliation period, 23–24
undefended divorce petition, 25
Affidavits: affidavit of means, 57–59, 61
application for *decree absolute*, 27
divorce petition requirements, 26–27, 29, 36
domestic violence procedure, 56
Northern Ireland divorce procedure, 111
Scotland divorce procedure, 110
Affiliation orders, 95
Aliment, 110–111
Assets *see* Capital assets
Assistance by way of representation, 100–101
Attachment of earnings orders, 64

Bank accounts, 73
Barristers: payment of legal fees, 98, 101
Behaviour: affidavit requirements, 26
six-month reconciliation period, 24
undefended divorce petition, 25
unreasonable behaviour grounds for divorce, 21, 22–23, 34
Bench warrant, 48
Benefits entitlement, 106–108
Bond: child return bond, 44
Building society accounts, 73

Calderbank letter, 106
Capital assets: affidavit of means, 58
capital gains tax, 85–86
effect on legal aid eligibility, 103
financial settlement, 84–85
Capital transfer tax, 86
Care and control order, 41–42
Certificate of civil legal aid, 101–102
Certificate of reconciliation, 24, 25
Certificate of satisfaction, 28, 37
Change of name procedure, 44
Child Abduction and Custody Act 1985, 49, 50
Children: access, 42–43; access disputes, 46–47; cost of access proceedings, 106
care and control order, 41–42
change of name, 44
child abduction, 47–51
child benefit, 108
custody, 30–31, 32; custody disputes, 44–47; cost of custody proceedings, 106; joint custody order, 40, 41; sole custody order, 40–41
holiday travel abroad, 43–44
judge's certificate of satisfaction, 28, 37
maintenance payments, 62, 63–65, 110–111; taxation, 63–68
statement of arrangements for children, 24, 25, 123–124
unmarried couples, 95–96
victims of domestic violence, 54
ward of court procedure, 48–49
Children Abroad Self-Help Group, 51
Children's Legal Centre, 51
Citizen's Advice Bureau, 14, 39, 54
Civil legal aid certificate, 101–102
Clean break financial settlement, 77

Cohabitation: factor affecting maintenance payments, 65
  legal situation, 93–96
Common law husbands and wives, 93–96
Conciliation: family conciliation services, 14, 39–40, 46, 47, 61; addresses, 115, 129–135
  in-court conciliation procedure, 40, 45, 46–47
Consent orders, 61
Co-respondent: adultery allegation, 22, 25
Costs: affidavit fees, 26, 36
  court proceedings costs, 105–106
  decree absolute certificate, 36
  divorce petition fee, 24, 36
  divorce proceedings, 105
  financial proceedings, 105
  fixed-fee interview, 19
  FLBA Conciliation Board, 61–62
  legal costs and aid, 97–108
Counselling services, 13–15, 17, 25
Courts: court fees, 98
  court proceedings costs, 105–106
  court welfare officer's role, 45, 46–47, 48
  defended divorce procedure, 31–32
  general divorce procedure, 35–38
  grounds for granting a divorce, 21
  grounds for not granting a divorce, 23–24
  in-court conciliation procedure, 40, 45, 46–47
  magistrates court maintenance claim, 72–73
  maintenance payments orders, 62–65
  presentation of divorce petition, 21
  protective powers, 54–56
  undefended divorce documents, 24–27, 32–33
  wardship procedure, 48–49
Cross petitions, 32
Custody: custody of children, 30–31, 32; custody disputes, 44–47; cost of custody proceedings, 106; joint custody order, 40, 41; sole custody order, 40–41

Death-in-service benefit, 90
Debts: affidavit of means, 58
  considered in financial settlement, 73
  household debt, 74
  insurance policy premiums, 74–75
  mortgage arrears, 75
  rent arrears, 75
Decree absolute: undefended divorce, 27–28, 36–37
Decree nisi: undefended divorce, 24–28, 36–37
Deed of separation, 33–34, 66–67, 127–128
Defended divorce, 31–32
Desertion: affidavit requirements, 26
  grounds for divorce, 21, 23
  undefended divorce petition, 26
Directions for trial form, 25
Divorce: defended divorce, 31–32
  divorce proceedings costs, 105
  foreign divorce decrees, 87–88
  handling procedure oneself, 35–38
  legal grounds for divorce, 21
  petition for divorce, 21, 121–126
  timescale of divorce, 32
  undefended divorce, 24–28
Documents: defended divorce requirements, 31–32
  divorce procedure requirements, 35–38
  financial application requirements, 59–60
  green form scheme, 99–100
  legal aid scheme requirements, 99–105
  undefended divorce requirements, 24–27, 32
Do-it-yourself divorce procedure, 35–38
Domicile: definition, 21–22
Domestic Proceedings and Magistrates Courts Act 1978, 55, 73
Domestic Violence Act 1978, 55
Domestic Violence and Matrimonial Proceedings Act 1976, 56

Education: school fees financial settlement, 91–92
  university grants, 92
Exclusion orders, 55
Expenditure: affidavit of means, 58–59

Family income supplement, 107
Family Law Bar Association Conciliation Board, 61
Family Law Association, 16; code of practice, 117–120
Fathers: care and control responsibility, 41–42
Finance: deed of separation arrangements, 34
  final financial agreement, 37–38, 61
  financial application procedure, 57–60
  financial orders in foreign divorces, 87–88

financial proceedings costs, 105
general financial arrangements, 57–88
importance of mutual agreement, 32–33, 35
information required by solicitor, 18–19, 139–141
maintenance payments, 28–30, 62–73
Foreign divorce decrees, 87–88
Forms *see* Documents

Green form scheme, 99–100
Guardianship of Minors Acts 1971 and 1973, 67

Holidays: children's access arrangements, 42–43
travelling abroad with children, 43–44
House: affidavit of means, 58
matrimonial home settlement, 78–86
property adjustment order, 30
registration of rights of occupation, 82–83
unmarried couples, 93–95
Household contents: financial settlement, 83–84

Income: affidavit of means, 57–58
checklist for income, 139–141
effect on legal aid eligibility, 102–103
income from lump sum payment, 77–78
Information needed by solicitor, 18–19
Inheritance (Provision for Family and Dependants) Act 1975, 96
Inheritance tax, 86
Injunctions: non-molestation injunctions, 54–56
ouster injunctions, 54–56
Inland Revenue: maintenance orders, 65–66, 68
school fees payments, 91–92
Institute of Family Therapy, 14; address, 133
Insurance policies: financial settlement arrangements, 90
provision against loss of pension rights, 89–90
responsibility for payment, 74–75
Ireland, Northern *see* Northern Ireland

Judicial separation, 33, 90

Land Registry, 82
Law Society: address, 114
examination of solicitor's bill, 98
general advice, 17
legal aid scheme, 19, 99–105

Lawyers *see* Solicitors
Legal aid: addresses of offices, 137–138
changing solicitors, 20
child abduction, 49, 50, 101
emergency legal aid, 49, 101–102
foreign legal aid schemes, 104
Legal Aid Scheme, 19, 99–105
payment of legal costs, 97–108
Scotland divorce procedure, 110
Legal costs *see* Costs
Liabilities: affidavit of means, 58
considered in financial settlement, 73
Lump sum orders, 29, 30, 77
Lump sum payment, 77–78, 89

Magistrates court maintenance claim, 72–73
Maintenance: calculating amount required, 68–72, 75–77
deed of separation, 33
general maintenance payments, 28–30, 62–65
magistrates court application, 72–73
maintenance pending suit, 28–29, 63–64
Scotland divorce procedure, 110–111
small maintenance payments, 67–68
tax implications of maintenance orders, 65–68
unmarried couples, 95–96
voluntary maintenance payments, 67
Marriage Guidance Council, 13–14, 17, 25
Married Women's Property Act 1882, 84, 90
Matrimonial and Family Proceedings Act 1984, 60, 75, 77, 87–88
Matrimonial Causes (Northern Ireland) Order 1978, 111
Matrimonial Homes Act 1983, 55, 75
Mediator lawyers, 15
Minute of order, 32
Mortgages: mortgage interest tax relief, 81–82, 95
responsibility for payment, 75, 81
Mothers: care and control responsibility, 41–42
right to maintenance, 75–76

National Family Conciliation Council, 39, 47, 115, 129–135
National Fostercare Association, 63, 115
National Marriage Guidance Council, 13–14, 17, 25
Non-molestation injunctions, 54–56
Northern Ireland: divorce procedure, 111

Northern Ireland – *cont.*
  effect of divorce on wills, 92
  legal aid scheme, 103–104

Orders: affiliation orders, 95
  attachment of earnings orders, 64
  consent orders, 61
  lump sum orders, 29, 30, 77
  periodical payments orders, 29, 30
  secured periodical payments orders, 29, 30
Ouster injunctions, 54–56

Pensions: loss of pension rights on divorce, 89–90
Periodical allowances, 110
Periodical payments orders, 29, 30
Petitioner: definition, 21
Petitions: cross petitions, 32
  defended divorce petitions, 31–32
  divorce petition fees, 24, 36
  petition for divorce, 21, 121–126
  prayer of the petition, 28, 30, 57, 122
  undefended divorce petition, 24–27
Police: child abduction procedure, 49–50
  protection against violence, 53
Prayer of the petition, 28, 30, 57, 122
Property: affidavit of means, 58
  matrimonial home settlement, 78–86
  property adjustment order, 30
  registration of rights of occupation, 82–83
  unmarried couples, 93–95
Protection orders, 55

Rates: responsibility for payment, 74
Reconciliation certificate, 24, 25
Registrar: role in custody and access disputes, 46–47
Remarriage: effect on wills, 92
  importance of *decree absolute*, 27–28, 36–37
Rent: responsibility for payment, 75
Residency: definition of domicile, 21–22
Respondent: definition, 21

School fees: financial settlement arrangements, 91–92
Scotland: divorce procedure, 109–111
  effect of divorce on wills, 92
  legal aid scheme, 103–104
Secured periodical payments orders, 29, 30
Seek and find orders, 48

Separation: affidavit requirements, 26–27
  deed of separation, 33–34, 66–67, 127–128
  grounds for divorce, 21, 23
  judicial separation, 33, 90
  six-month reconciliation period, 24
  undefended divorce petition, 25
Sherdley v. Sherdley, 92
Six-month reconciliation period, 23–24
Small maintenance payments, 67–68
Solicitors: changing solicitors, 19–20
  domestic violence procedure, 54, 56
  early consultation, 15–16
  family lawyers, 16–17
  financial agreement advice, 38
  first interview, 17–19
  fixed-fee interview, 19
  mediator lawyers, 15
  payment of legal costs, 97–108
  presentation of divorce petition, 22
  'taxation of a bill' procedure, 98–99
Solicitors' Family Law Association, 16;
  code of practice, 117–120
Stamp duty on property transfer, 82
Statutory charge, 104–105
Supplementary benefit, 95, 106–107

Taxation: capital gains tax on sale of assets, 85–86
  capital gains tax on sale of house, 81, 85
  capital transfer tax, 86
  deed of separation, 33–34
  inheritance tax, 86
  maintenance payments, 65–68, 110–111
  mortgage interest tax relief, 81–82, 95
  school fees tax relief, 91–92
  'taxation of a bill', 98–99

Undefended divorce, 24–28
United States: mediator lawyers, 15
University grants, 92
Unmarried couples: legal situation, 93–96
Unreasonable behaviour *see* Behaviour

Violence: procedures to obtain protection, 53–56
Voluntary maintenance payments, 67

Ward of Court procedure, 48–49
Wills: effects of divorce, 92